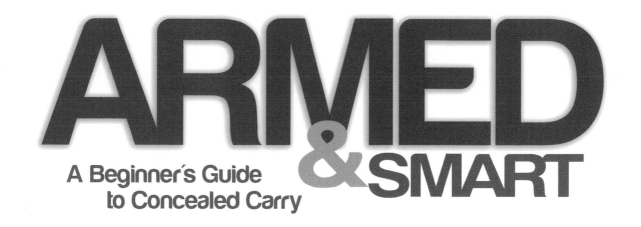

ARMED
&SMART

A Beginner's Guide
to Concealed Carry

**David Bahde,
Paul Markel
& Terrill Hoffman**

ARMED AND SMART

Authors:

David Bahde is a fulltime firearms instructor, tactical consultant and writer. His work regularly appears on Tactical-Life.com and in *Guns & Weapons for Law Enforcement*, among others. He wrote chapters 3, 5, 7, 11 and 13 for this book.

Terrill Hoffman operates Terrill Hoffman Photography and moderates Knifeforums.com. His writing concerning both knives and firearms frequently appears in Harris Outdoor Magazine's various publications. He wrote chapters 2, 8, 9, 14 and 15 for this book.

Paul Markel is the host of the Sportsman Channel's series *Student of the Gun* and operates the Student of the Gun University training program. He has extensive military and law enforcement experience and now spends much of his time writing about firearm technique and safety for various publications. He wrote chapters 1, 4, 6, 10 and 12 for this book.

Providing Photography:

David Bahde, Terrill Hoffman, Craig Lamb, Paul Markel, Laurie Tisdale, National Shooting Sports Foundation, Hornady and Smith & Wesson.

Cover photo by Oleg Volk

ARMED AND SMART

© 2014 Whitman Publishing, LLC
3101 Clairmont Road • Suite G • Atlanta, GA 30329

ARMED AND SMART
ISBN: 0794842054   EAN: 9780794842055

Correspondence concerning this book may be direct to the publisher.

Printed in the United States of America.

Contents

VI

Foreword

As a proud gun owner, I feel honored Second Amendment Media has asked me to write the forward for this book, *Armed and Smart*. Primarily, I hope to encourage readers to enter the political discourse concerning gun control and gun ownership. As a mother, educator and firearms enthusiast, I trust those who read this book will gain a deeper understanding of handguns and the importance of protecting our right to own firearms. By not actively participating in the civil discussion over gun control, one, by default, supports those who wish to forbid Americans to own and use firearms. While firearms deserve respect and a certain amount of precaution, they offer law abiding citizens an unmatched level of freedom and security. The current political climate and my job necessitates I obscure my identity, but I've included three instances from my life that have furthered my belief in firearm ownership and concealed carry: 1) living in a country that forbids citizens from owning firearms, 2) finding myself without a gun in compromising situations and 3) encountering an "active shooter" criminal while working in a gun-free zone.

"You never want to live in a country where the only people with guns are the government."
~Gerald L. Montgomery

At age 25, I moved to Japan for three years. While I love traveling and experiencing different cultures, my real joy in Japan came from speaking with locals about their everyday lives. One particular conversation and event has stuck with me over the years more so than others. One morning, Kazuko, our mama-san, a nanny of sorts, and I drove by a group of Japanese men carrying signs and walking circles in front of a local business. Kazuko explained the men were protesting their employer, but could only do so between 7:00 and 8:00 a.m. before returning to work. She told me that was "...all they could do." This scene stands as a testament to the Japanese government's control over its people. The Japanese government slowly began banning firearm ownership and other rights after WW II, and the Japanese people must now follow a strict set of rules that strip them of their freedoms. As Americans, we should protect all of our civil liberties to ensure we never fall victim to such harsh governmental control.

A well-regulated Militia, being necessary to the security of a free state, the right of the people to keep and bear Arms, shall not be infringed.

~2nd Amendment

One evening after attending one of my daughter's softball games, she and I stopped at a less than desirable motel in a small West Tennessee town. We checked in a little after midnight and, as we approached our room, encountered four men gathered around the walkway to our door. The men were half-naked and drunk. As we tried to pass by them, the men wouldn't move and made us squeeze through them to our room. While they didn't assault us, their threatening demeanor established they

(Continued)

could overpower us if they chose. Before I closed the door to our room, I turned around and locked eyes with the oldest member of the group. I gave him a long, hard look, letting him know I would remember his face if they tried harming us. That night I doubt I slept a wink. Though nothing else happened, these drunk, aggressive men had us at their mercy. If they decided to kick down our door and attack us, we couldn't have stopped them. From then on, I swore to never go without a firearm to alleviate my fears if I or my family ever encountered another situation where we were nearly physically helpless.

When the well is dry, we know the wealth of water. ~ Ben Franklin

I've lived my whole life around guns. My grandparents, father, brothers, and friends have all regularly hunted and shot targets. While never having a problem with guns, for an extended period of my life I didn't feel compelled to own or carry a firearm. It didn't seem needed, given my lifestyle. But, my stance towards guns changed drastically on February 10th, 2010. I was working at a public elementary school in East Tennessee and that day witnessed a co-worker shoot the school's two principals. I was standing four feet away on the other side of a thin office door at the time of the shooting and quickly took cover under a desk to call 911. As I talked to the 911 operator, the gunman walked from the principal's office to the desk where I had taken cover, huddling over two 6-year-old students. At that moment, I couldn't do anything to defend myself against the gunman. Given current laws, my legally-owned and permitted gun was at home, leaving me defenseless. My life was completely in his hands and I'm only alive today because he decided to end his shooting spree. Remarkably, both principals survived and the police apprehended the gunman, who is now spending the rest of his life in prison. While most people at the school that day have put the incident behind them, I can't shake the fact my fate depended on a man who'd just shot my two supervisors. Since then, I've taken steps to ensure I can protect my right to life from another such attack. My fate is now my own.

While I like to believe those trying to pass stricter gun laws have good intentions, these detractors fail to admit bad people won't adhere to laws and these same laws won't protect the innocent from harm. Because those who argue against firearms won't recognize the wickedness, insanity, twisted nature of some people, they often become the first to give up their freedoms. Thus, as you read, please consider the importance of owning and carrying a firearm.

Sincerely,
-A neighbor, teacher and friend

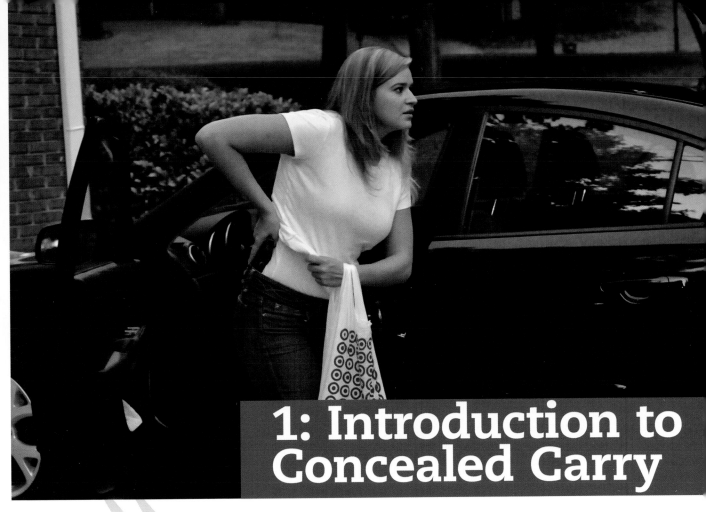

1: Introduction to Concealed Carry

Handgun ownership is a legal right of law-abiding Americans. For some, owning a handgun provides a reassuring level of security at home. Others take that ownership outside of the home. They are part of a growing population of Americans exercising the right for concealed-carry use of a handgun.

While carrying a handgun in public is certainly a significant decision, gun owners should feel confident pursuing the proper means to carry a gun. Certain media and political organizations only promote the dangers of firearms. Carrying a handgun stems from a responsibility one feels to protect themselves and those around them.

This book hopes to encourage and equip new gun owners with the skills and knowledge to safely bring their weapon in public

and defend themselves from harm or worse. A handgun can't provide defense if stored away or not with its owner, so we aim to detail the information one needs to feel secure carrying a weapon for protection against life threatening situations.

States often require those who wish to carry a weapon to apply for a carry concealed carry permit, which indicates a citizen has stayed within good standing of the law and gone through the proper instruction and training to use and keep a gun on their person. Some may argue carrying or keeping a firearm in the home is paranoid or asking for trouble, but in reality guns offer an unparalleled amount of security for those who've gone through the effort to familiarize themselves with their weapon.

Fire Extinguisher Mentality

Firearms skeptics often wrongly assume that people only carry a handgun with the desire to use the weapon for uses beyond personal defense. While firearms have their risks, detractors fail to realize that owning and carrying a handgun is a preventive measure, much like a fire extinguisher kept under the sink or in the trunk of a car. Similarly, concealed weapons can protect the innocent from an unexpected threat, but one should only use them as a last resort against those threatening their life and wellbeing. Additionally, those who own or carry a gun should never bring their weapon into public as an act of aggression or purposefully enter a dangerous situation with hopes of discharging their firearm.

Carrying a firearm is similar to having insurance. You don't know what could happen, but you are prepared in case you find yourself in a life-threatening situation.

Concealed firearms help ensure bad things don't happen to good people. A concealed weapon equalizes all people when law enforcement cannot protect one's right to life.

When You Might Need It

To the newcomer in the firearm's world, the thought of carrying a concealed weapon can certainly seem daunting. Some get their concealed carry permit, but feel apprehensive about carrying a gun and begin finding ways to justify leaving it at home.

While carrying a gun can cause common and healthy amounts of nervousness, one should overcome personal reservations and carry a weapon wherever the law allows. When one decides to carry their gun only when they believe they need it, two unique problems arise that remain too significant to ignore. First, no one ever knows where danger might strike. Not to sound alarmist or paranoid, but no one can faithfully predict where and when a threat might occur requiring the use of a firearm.

Additionally, only sporadically carrying a firearm could present a handful of unwanted legal troubles. If an assailant causes a permit carrier to discharge his or her weapon, lawyers could make the case that the permit carrier intentionally brought his or her weapon in public to harm the assailant, as the permit holder didn't normally carry the weapon. Thus, the lawyer could call the permit holder's motives into question and even assert the shooting was premeditated and not an act of defense. To stay above reproach and avoid unfair legal hassles, those with concealed carry permits should always keep their gun on hand and establish a rapport as a regular gun carrier.

The Kel-Tec P3AT semi-auto pistol stands as the most lightweight .380 ACP currently in production. Upon its release, the P3AT became one of the first pocket sized pistols to fire .380 ACP rounds. Weighing only 8.3oz unloaded, the gun features a six round magazine and is similar in size to many .22 caliber pocket pistols.

3

Many firearm experts cite the Kel-Tec P3AT as starting the modern .380 and 9mm pocket pistol trend.

The Reality of Concealed Carry

The bitter truth of carrying a concealed weapon is that sometimes the world is an ugly place. Good, honest people require little governing, but bad people, despite any laws our government may pass, are nearly impossible to govern at all. Because of this, carrying a weapon has become a sobering but needed level of security for many people. Crime isn't exclusive to seedy neighborhoods or darkened alleyways, but can happen anywhere and to anyone. Every day assailants and criminals harm the unsuspecting and the ill-prepared, but carrying a concealed weapon minimizes this threat and allows individuals to stand against those who wish to impose on their right to life, health and happiness. We hope those who carry a concealed weapon never have to use it, but one should also have the means to defend themselves if necessary. While we wish the world was always safe, we must unfortunately recognize wicked people exist and could harm anyone at anytime.

One should only fire their weapon if certain an assailant would otherwise end their or another bystander's life. Those carrying a concealed firearm should never fire their weapon to scare away what they might perceive as a potential attack.

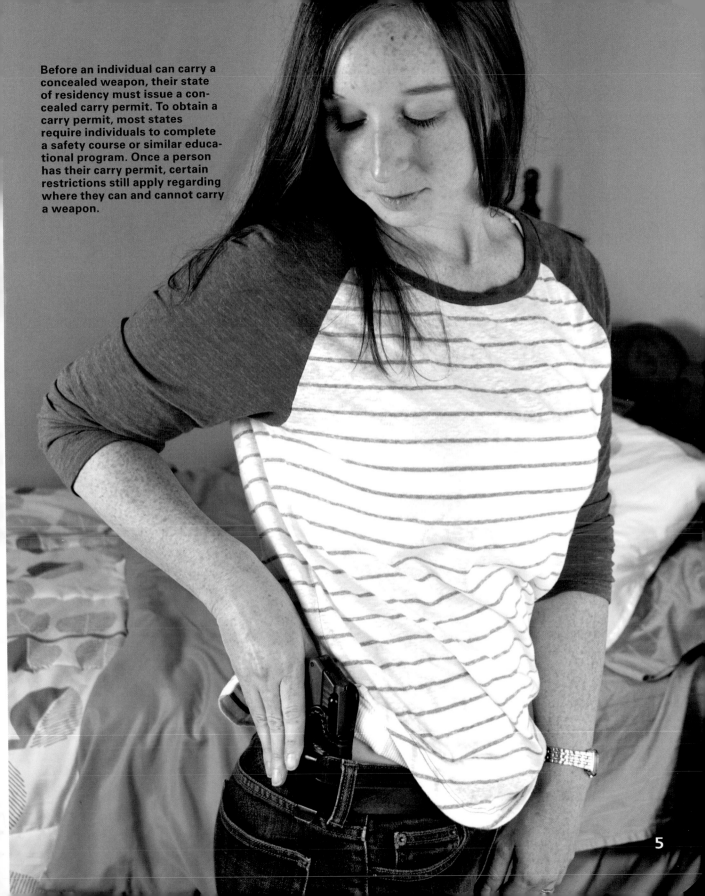

Before an individual can carry a concealed weapon, their state of residency must issue a concealed carry permit. To obtain a carry permit, most states require individuals to complete a safety course or similar educational program. Once a person has their carry permit, certain restrictions still apply regarding where they can and cannot carry a weapon.

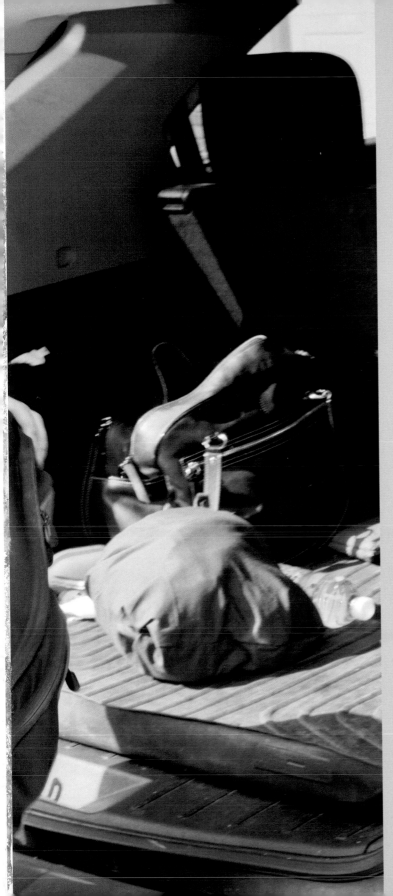

Concealed Carry Mentality

Over the last several decades, members of law enforcement have adopted the term "getting burned" to signify when criminals discover an undercover police officer's handgun. While getting "burned" typically applies to cops blowing their cover, those new to carrying a concealed weapon often have a similar experience, believing everyone in public can see their weapon. Those with a concealed weapon may think everyone notices their weapon the first time they step out of the house and that it's obvious they have a gun hidden on their body. While a certain amount of nervousness can be expected when first bringing a gun in public, those who think everyone can notice their weapon often believe strangers are more observant than they are in reality. Most people in public focus on their own thoughts and don't spend a large amount of time noticing others. Typically strangers only notice people who really stand out and even if they do notice a person's gun, wouldn't likely say anything as long as the situation remains neutral and non-threatening. Those with their carry permit should rest assured that carrying their weapon in public is within the confines of the law and usually goes completely unnoticed. To test to see if a stranger can identify the outline of a gun underneath your clothing, secure your gun on your person then ask a friend or a spouse if they notice anything different about you. If it takes them a few minutes to see it or if they can't spot the gun at all, in all likelihood you could assume no one in public would notice the gun either. Try standing in various positions and making different movements to see if your gun becomes more or less noticeable.

Amendment II

A well regulated Militia, being necessary to the security of a free State, the right of the people to keep and bear Arms, shall not be infringed.

While only one sentence, the Second Amendment to the Constitution remains one of the most misunderstood aspects of American legal doctrine. Given most of us probably haven't taken a civics or history class in years, we can easily forget the implications of this amendment and what it means "to keep and bear arms." To understand the Second Amendment, we must first study its context within and alongside the Declaration of Independence, the U.S. Constitution and the Bill of Rights. Before carrying a firearm, those with a concealed carry permit should review these documents and study how they still influence gun ownership.

The right to bear arms gives citizens the ability to defend the nation.

9

America's citizen militia joined uniformed troops to win independence from the occupying British.

Declaring our Independence

The Declaration of Independence states the founding principles of our government and stands as the cornerstone of American freedom. In the process of rebelling from British rule and forging an independent union, Thomas Jefferson, who wrote much of the document, ensured the Declaration of Independence guaranteed the individual rights of man. In stating the beliefs of our founding fathers, the Declaration of Independence reads: "We hold these truths to be self-evident, that all men are created equal, that they are endowed by their Creator with certain unalienable Rights, that among these are Life, Liberty, and the pursuit of Happiness."

These few lines state that all persons have a set of rights endowed by God that a government or another man cannot infringe upon. While U.S. citizens would eventually enjoy many more rights than those outlined in the Declaration of Independence, the document asserts citizens' basic freedoms and introduces man's right to existence, which would become the principle behind self-defense laws.

Interestingly enough, the U.S. Constitution doesn't mention or grant any individual rights to American citizens. The Constitution's first three articles establish our government, outlining the Legislative, Executive and Judicial branches and the respective system of checks and balances between them. The Fourth and Sixth articles address the relationship of power between the Federal and State Governments. Additionally, the Fifth outlines amending the Constitution, while the Seventh ratifies it into law.

The Colt Commander is a mid-sized semi-automatic pistol and a shorter variant of the full-size 1911 designed by John M. Browning. The pistol is available in several different calibers, such as 9mm, .38 Super and .45 ACP. Due to the design's inherent slim width, the .45 ACP, shown below, remains a popular conceal and carry choice today.

 The right to bear arms guarantees our government remains for the people, as citizens (given enough support) could form militias and overthrow any dictator if necessary.

Bill of Rights

The Bill of Rights stand as the first ten amendments to the Constitution and primarily address individual freedoms. Adopted in 1791, these amendments limit the Federal Government's power over citizens and individual states. With the British occupation still fresh in their minds, the colonies passed the Bill of Rights to ensure the government didn't overstep its bounds. The Second Amendment notes that the U.S. Government, unlike British forces, could never strip law abiding citizens of their firearms, a law that thus guaranteed another country could never occupy our nation and citizens could overthrow the government if necessary.

Our Founding Fathers had the wisdom and foresight to recognize that governments don't always act in its citizens' best interest and they created the Bill of Rights to further guarantee the right to life and self-evident freedoms. Because of the Bill of Rights, Americans today can keep weapons in their home and, after going through the proper procedures, carry a weapon in public to defend their inalienable right to life against those who wish to infringe upon that freedom.

The Right to Bear Arms

When examining the Declaration of Independence, the Bill of Rights and ultimately the Second Amendment, one can understand the importance and historical significance of the right to bear arms. While most states honor the Constitution's sanctity and preserve individuals' rights to own and carry firearms, the last several decades have seen a host of cities and states infringe upon these rights and heavily restrict or even ban firearms. Many have unfortunately come to believe that firearms only exist to cause harm and negatively affect our country and have thus re-interpreted the Constitution to align with their own beliefs. Firearms certainly demand a fair amount of respect and one should use discretion when carrying and using one, but firearms help secure our liberty and stand as one of the great equalizers in our country.

Many of the detractors against firearms have a narrow understanding of the intent behind the Bill of Rights. If these skeptics lived in an era of political oppression like our forefathers experienced, they'd likely better understand the role and importance of firearms and how the right to bear arms remains as important today as during the forging of our country. To a lesser extent, one could even take someone unfamiliar with firearms to the shooting range and demonstrate proper gun etiquette, proving that guns, when used properly, play a needed part in our society.

Just the Facts

As mentioned, a host of cities and states have passed laws restricting the use or banning firearms. One can try to optimistically assume politicians passed these laws with good intentions, but regardless, the restrictions often cause more harm than they do good and they do not better peoples' lives. The first significant firearms ban occurred in 1934, when Congress passed the National Firearms Act. The law intended to curb the use and manufacturing of fully automatic machine guns and short barrel shotguns, which gangsters favored and widely used. The law later went under several revisions, but many of its anti-gun dogmas still linger in U.S. law.

The Federal Assault Weapons Ban came in 1994, again with the intent of restricting citizens of their individual rights and freedoms. The AWB labeled certain semi-automatic guns illegal based on cosmetic features, including the AR-15, the Beretta AR-70 and the FN FAL rifles. The law passed under the assumption that because these weapons resemble fully automatic, military grade rifles, they pose a threat to the public welfare and civilians should not have access to them.

The AWB expired in 2004 and companies have again begun manufacturing these weapons. Studies have shown that the ban on semi-automatic assault-style rifles did little to affect gun violence across the country and thus proved ineffective and rendered citizens less prepared to defend themselves. Though the AWB has since become defunct, countless firearm laws exist across the country. Before purchasing or carrying a concealed weapon, one should familiarize themselves with their local laws or take a concealed carry class that will outline local ordinances. A local police department, gun shop or attorney general can point one in the direction of these classes or local laws. The gun world openly embraces newcomers, so one should set aside any reservations or concerns about seeking out these professionals.

Choosing the right caliber may seem like a daunting task, but it's important to keep it simple and choose the correct round for the individual shooter. First and foremost, no special type of caliber or gun can replace proper training and accurate shot placement. It's important to choose the largest caliber one can effectively manage, but this will vary from person to person. The latter portion of this book discusses bullets and ammunition in great detail, but for now the topic needs some clarity. Different calibers provide different levels of protection during an attack. Though somewhat bleak to think about, most experts would agree rounds that can quickly penetrate and expand in an attacker's vital organs offer the best level of defense in the event of an attack. Those with their carry permit should only use their weapon if an assailant has placed lives at stake, thus a round must stop an assailant in order to keep innocent people out of harm's way.

Those carrying a concealed firearm must pick a weapon lethal enough to neutralize an assailant but small enough to easily and comfortably conceal.

Caliber choices

Caliber is defined as the diameter of the projectile or bullet. Many factors contribute in deciding the best caliber for an individual and, while important, the size of the bullet should not act as the only deciding factor when choosing a caliber. Different calibers have differing powder loads and these powder loads change the overall energy produced by a round. The simplest way to understand a bullet's on-target effectiveness is to determine its muzzle energy or, simply, the kinetic energy of the round. Knowing the muzzle energy simply helps understand the relation of the bullet's speed (velocity) to its weight (mass). Bullet weight and velocity remain equally important. Just because a bullet is faster and has a greater velocity, doesn't necessarily mean it's better or more effective. For example: would you rather be hit by a dump truck at 30 miles per hour or be hit by a beach ball at 90 miles per hour? Although the lighter of the two has a higher velocity, the heavier object will cause far more damage. Many manufacturers include muzzle energy on the back of the ammunition box. However, this can be calculated using the standard kinetic energy formula: $KE = \frac{1}{2}MV^2$ where energy equals ½ mass times velocity squared.

Typically, higher energy calibers will cause more felt recoil and muzzle climb, making properly handling the gun and taking fast follow-up shots more difficult. Again, it's important to

.357 Magnum

.38 Special, .40 caliber and .45 ACP

9mm

choose a caliber that is manageable to the shooter and practices accurate shot placement. It's also important to realize that bullets can penetrate through multiple walls and other objects, which can be good or bad depending on the situation. Higher energy bullets typically penetrate through more objects while frangible or some hollow point rounds penetrate less.

Gun critics and enthusiasts typically group calibers into three main categories: low, medium and high energy. Sub-categories exist within each caliber based on powder load and bullet weight. Many calibers fall into more than one of the main categories as variations in powder load and bullet type affect energy. Manufacturers offer the most popular calibers, such as the .380, .38, 9mm, .40 and .45, in subsonic, standard, +P and a few other variations. Subsonic rounds are used primarily for suppressed fire, as they travel slower than the speed of sound and therefore do not produce the loud 'crack' made by faster bullets breaking the sound barrier. Shooters primarily use standard rounds for practice and target shooting, as they're typically cheaper and easy to shoot. The +P rounds are primarily made for self defense, as they're loaded with more powder and typically have more energy than their standard counterparts. When carrying a handgun, it's important to utilize the self-defense type of ammunition, as it's designed to expand upon impact and provide a higher chance of eliminating the target without over penetrating into something or someone behind the target.

Ultimately, choose the caliber that best suits your needs, can be easily handled and is available in a self-defense variation that can accurately and consistently place shots on target.

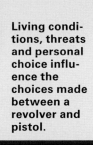

S&W M&P

Living conditions, threats and personal choice influence the choices made between a revolver and pistol.

.38 Special

Pistols and revolvers

Breaking down the choices by handgun category keeps things simple. For the sake of clarity, pistols are generally referred to in the gun world as semi-automatics. Semi-autos typically come in full sized, compact, and sub-compact variations. Manufactures typically place revolvers in a stand-alone category separate from pistols.

Gun enthusiasts and historians typically define a pistol as a handgun with a chamber integral with the barrel. Semi-automatics have become the most popular type of pistol and favored by shooters for the quick succession of rounds they can fire. Ammunition is loaded into a magazine and inserted into the magazine well, typically located in the pistol's grip. A mech-

anism loads a fresh cartridge into the chamber and extracts the spent casing each time the shooter presses the trigger. This allows the user to fire an entire magazine of ammunition before reloading.

Unlike a pistol, revolvers rely on a rotating cylinder with multiple chambers to move rounds into the firing position and their chambers aren't fixed to the barrel. Many revolvers have six chambers in the cylinder, but this may vary with size and caliber.

The revolver allows the user to fire multiple rounds before reloading. The cylinder revolves to

align with the next chamber each time the shooter cocks the hammer.

In a single-action revolver, the shooter pulls the hammer back with a free hand or thumb and squeezes the trigger to release the hammer. In a double-action revolver, the hammer is moved back by the trigger in one motion when the shooter pulls the trigger back before the gun fires. A double-action revolver can also fire as single-action by manually cocking the hammer if the revolver has an exposed hammer.

Chapter 6 of this book further details semi-automatic pistols and their various firing mechanisms.

Full-Sized Pistols

Manufacturers design full-sized pistols for duty use, as they are often carried by law enforcement officers, security professionals and special operators. Barrel lengths for full-sized pistols range from 4 to 6 inches. Longer barrels generally result in more velocity and less recoil. Full-sized pistols with longer barrels have a longer sight radius, which is the distance between the front sight and the rear sight. A longer sight radius allows the shooter more precise sight alignment.

Full-sized pistols tend to be heavier. The added weight helps manage recoil and muzzle climb, but smaller framed individuals may find them difficult to wield. Full-sized pistols typically have larger grips to better accommodate handling and increase ammunition capacity.

Concealing a full-sized pistol takes greater thought and effort. Some concealed-carry holders prefer to carry as large a pistol as practical.

Full-sized pistols remain very popular for concealed carry, among these the M1911. The 1911 fires .45-ACP rounds and is a single-action, semi-automatic, magazine-fed and recoil-operated pistol. The U.S. armed forces issued the 1911 as its standard sidearm from 1911 until 1985.

The 1911 continues to have a strong following. Many manufacturers now produce their own version of this pistol. Overall construction is largely the same, making brand less critical on quality pistols. Most full-sized 1911 pistols use 5-inch barrels and their magazine's typically have an eight round capacity. Pistols chambered in 9mm and other calibers have increased in popularity, as they can hold more ammunition than their .45-ACP counterparts.

Manufacturers typically offer the 1911 as a single-action and when cocked, the hammer stays pulled back, leading to the advent of the term "cocked and locked." When the shooter fires the gun, the trigger releases and brings the hammer forward. The gun features a safety in the grip, requiring the shooter to have the pistol firmly in hand before firing.

Although safe to carry, the appearance of the 1911 remains an issue for many carrying concealed weapons. Steel versions of the gun are heavy while alloy versions reduce the overall weight. Even so, thin slides allow easier use of inside-the-waistband (IWB) holsters.

Manipulating the safety is critical. That requires specialized training, but once mastered the 1911 makes an excellent choice for concealed carry.

There are many other makes and models of full-size pistols on the market. For those desiring a hammer that does not remain cocked, there are several pistols using a de-cocker mechanism. A lever on the side of the pistol safely drops the hammer forward with no need for a grip safety.

Typically referred to as a double action/single action (DA/SA), the first trigger pull is longer and generally takes more effort. Double action means it's both cocking and releasing the hammer in the same trigger pull. Follow up shots are fired in single action and require

Full-sized pistols with a longer sight radius give shooters an advantage in accuracy and velocity.

Beretta Model 92 clone made by Taurus.

less pressure on the trigger. These pistols must be de-cocked prior to holstering for safe carry.

Sig Sauer makes a number of these pistols. Other brand names include Heckler & Koch, Smith & Wesson, Beretta and others. Slight variations include a double action only (DAO) that removes the de-cocking lever. This action results in a heavier trigger pull that's the same every time.

Manufacturers offer other popular full-size pistols with a striker fired mechanism and made of lightweight polymer materials.

Striker-fired pistols remove the exposed hammer and most external safeties or de-cockers. Glock makes more full-sized versions of these firearms than most other manufacturers. A polymer frame brings lighter weight while the sturdy slide is made of steel. The full-size 9mm versions hold high-capacity 17-round magazines. Simple, reliable operation makes striker-fired pistols most popular with law enforcement officers and other armed professionals.

The Smith & Wesson M&P stands as another excellent example that can come with an external thumb safety. Some law enforcement agencies require an external safety as well as a magazine safety and the M&P fits both needs. Many who carry concealed firearms favor the gun, as it comes with interchangeable grips. The popular Springfield Armory XD even adds a grip safety for more control.

Striker-fired polymer pistols are lighter and provide an advantage for all-day carry with less strain when compared to pistols made of steel. Shooters have recognized these pistols for their high-capacity magazines, accuracy and reliability.

19

Striker-fired pistols

Striker-fired pistols are lighter and easier to carry for an extended period of time, as they weigh less than all-steel pistols. With that, their increased width could make concealment more problematic. These pistols make up for their increased width with capacity, accuracy and reliability. These popular high-capacity pistols utilize a unique firing mechanism that provides a safe, effective and durable operation for an ever-growing populace of gun owners.

With its high-capacity and smaller design, the Glock 19 9mm proves to be a popular carry pistol.

Kahr produces several concealed carry, striker-fired models designed for easy concealment and maximum firepower.

Compact Pistols

Manufacturers often design compact pistols after their full-sized counterparts. Compact pistols often feature barrel lengths ranging between 3 and 4 inches and shorter or the same grip diameters. The pistol's small frame reduces ammo capacity by a few rounds in conventional calibers, though the gun's operating controls remain identical.

Officers often carry these pistols as off duty versions of their duty weapons. Compact pistols may have increased recoil, flash and noise, depending on caliber.

Civilians often carry compact pistols for self-defense protection. The guns offer better concealment with less weight than full-sized versions. Other benefits include adequate capacity, solid reliability and ease of operation.

Compact pistols encompass almost every pistol design made today and most offer the same operating controls as their full-sized versions. Compact 1911 pistols with 3.5- and 4.25-inch barrels are common and most accept full-sized magazines, providing for

dual use with full-sized handguns. Any loss in velocity is minimal while gaining more concealment.

Compact versions of full-sized de-cocking pistols have also become popular. They remain the first choice for many law enforcement and military units. Sig Sauer has a large selection. Beretta, Heckler & Koch and CZ USA offer a number of logical choices. Many of these models are designed without sharp edges and specifically for concealed carry. They come with smoothed-out triggers and various sighting systems.

Striker fired pistols comprise the largest portion of this category. Major manufacturers make compact versions of their full-sized models. Most have shorter barrels and grips. Capacity is reduced but overall feel is similar to the full-sized version.

Sights are similar, controls are identical and overall operation stays the same. Recoil tends to increase depending on caliber, but they remain effective and easier to conceal. Examples are the Smith & Wesson M&P Compact and the Glock Compact models.

So many variations in size have caused the lines to blur when distinguishing between compact pistols and sub-compact pistols. Generally, a compact pistol's grip is large enough for the whole hand. Because of its size, a shooter's bottom one or two fingers might not fit on the grip without a finger extension on a special magazine. Manufacturers design compact pistols to have the functionality of a full-size pistol in a smaller package, but designed for concealment.

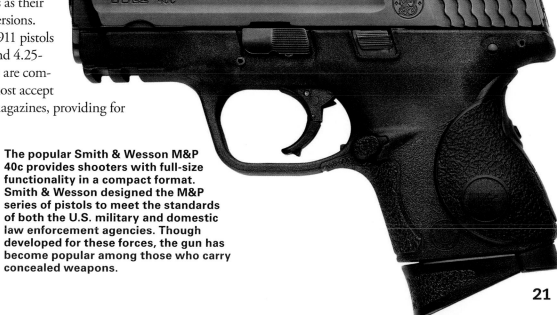

The popular Smith & Wesson M&P 40c provides shooters with full-size functionality in a compact format. Smith & Wesson designed the M&P series of pistols to meet the standards of both the U.S. military and domestic law enforcement agencies. Though developed for these forces, the gun has become popular among those who carry concealed weapons.

The Kel-Tec P3AT can fit within the palm of most full grown adults. Because of its size and the calibers it fires, the gun can effectively neutralize a threat, but some may find managing its recoil difficult. The gun comes in a variety of different colors, such as olive drab green as shown, that can accommodate most concealed carry scenarios.

Sub-compact handguns

Many will find sub-compact the easiest type of handgun to conceal. Many new designs come chambered in 9mm, .40 caliber and .45 ACP and handguns in those calibers provide adequate power and reliability while remaining highly concealable. The .380 ACP is a shorter version of the conventional 9mm round and common among sub-compacts.

Manufacturers have begun designing sub-compacts smaller and smaller. They can accommodate smaller calibers such as the .32 ACP, .25 Auto and .22 Long Rifle with barrel lengths as short as one inch, sometimes called 'pocket pistols.'

These small-framed guns easily fit in a pocket, which makes them convenient for concealed carry. However, due to their small size, one might find properly handling these guns difficult and aiming their shorter sights more difficult beyond close range.

Those new to concealed carry may find sub-compacts practical and easier to carry and conceal than larger, more bulky versions. These small guns leave no excuse for not carrying a handgun when an individual is "only going to the grocery store" or "only going to get gas."

The Kel-Tec P3AT, chambered for the .380 cartridge, remains a favorite for many because of its size, reliability, affordability and light weight. The P3AT is referred to by many as "the lightest .380 ACP pistol in the world."

Sub-compact semi-autos

Many will find sub-compact pistols best suited for extreme concealed carry. Some are shortened versions of full-sized pistols. Many are smaller and chambered in a variety of calibers. The .380, 9mm, .40 and .45 are all common in sub-compacts.

Those seeking to carry a weapon could consider the Colt Mustang .380 and Sig Sauer P238 as good single-action choices. Likewise, one could easily conceal the Ruger LCP, Smith & Wesson M&P Shield, Glock 26 and the

Springfield XD-S given their light-weight polymer designs. Beretta also makes quality sub-compacts in .22LR, .25ACP and .380.

Single and double-barrel models also fit into this category. They load by opening and closing the barrel. Some may find these guns challenging to aim, but their few moving parts make them reliable at close range.

The thin and small size of the sub-compact pistols make them easy to conceal in a handbag or pocket.

Revolvers

Revolvers remain in their own separate category for simplicity. They can fit into every category. Concealed carry revolvers offer simplistic reliability with no moving slide, magazine or need for external safety. As a rule, revolvers used for concealed carry have shorter barrels measuring 3 inches or less.

Shooters may have difficulty firing a revolver with full-power loads. They can have punishing recoil and require more training for better accuracy. Short barreled snub-nosed revolvers in .357 Magnum, .44 Special or even .45 ACP can remain effective, but shooters may find them difficult to carry and fire with accuracy.

Most revolvers used for concealment are chambered in .38 special or .357 Magnum. Differences in revolvers revolve around weight, barrel length and hidden or exposed hammers. Use of alloys and other metals make them very lightweight. Typically, the lighter the revolver, the more the recoil you'll feel.

While capacity is limited, operation is simple and reliable. Sighting at anything but close range is difficult and accuracy beyond 15 yards requires significant skill. For those willing to put in the training, they remain a popular concealed carry option.

Sub-compact revolvers

Concealed-carry revolvers offer simplistic reliability with no moving slide, magazine or need for external safety. Most use barrels of 2.5 inches or less while limiting magazine capacity to five rounds.

Many permit holders can conceal short barreled, full-sized revolvers and most are chambered in .357 Magnum or .38 Special. The latter caliber remains the most popular for concealed carry because of reduced noise, recoil and easier handling.

These revolvers have either exposed or covered hammers. Most prefer a covered hammer if carried in a purse or pocket, to prevent accidental snagging. On the downside, the hammer takes considerable effort to pull. Sights are short, sometimes hard to see and the gun more challenging to aim.

Another caliber choice that has become popular for concealed carry is the .32 H&R Magnum, and its big brother, the .327 Magnum. The .32 caliber family of rimmed cartridges has a long history going back more than a century to greats like the .32 S&W and others.

Vist Tactical-Life.com for the latest firearm reviews and news.

Conclusion

Those new to carrying a concealed weapon should place a lot of emphasis on the gun they purchase to bring in public. Doing so influences your interest in carry, practice and application for years to come. Too often those who start carrying a concealed weapon stop because they find their handgun too heavy, bulky or difficult to shoot. Those with their concealed permit should carry a gun they find comfortable and suits their preferences.

It takes time getting comfortable with frequently carrying a concealed weapon. Some find it easy to carry a full-sized pistol weighing 3 pounds, while others find such a gun uncomfortable and instead would prefer a lighter, more compact gun. Some who carry concealed weapons don't mind sacrificing some firepower for comfort.

All who have their carry permit should take time ensure they will actually bring the gun in public and shoot it with confidence and accuracy. Most importantly, enjoy shooting your handgun. Choose a gun you will like practicing with and carry, as both remain equally important. Handguns come in countless different makes and models and thus leave no excuse for not getting the weapon that best fits your needs and application.

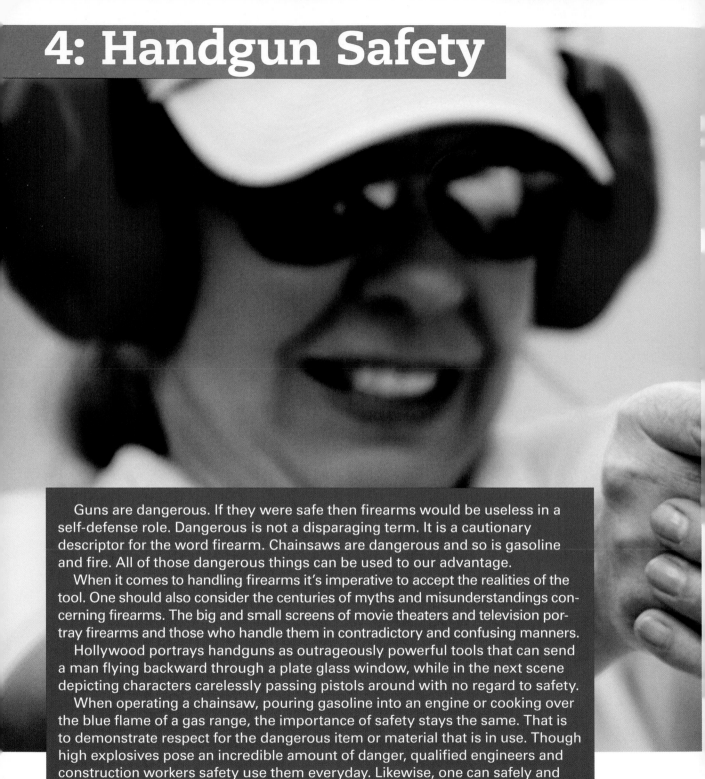

4: Handgun Safety

Guns are dangerous. If they were safe then firearms would be useless in a self-defense role. Dangerous is not a disparaging term. It is a cautionary descriptor for the word firearm. Chainsaws are dangerous and so is gasoline and fire. All of those dangerous things can be used to our advantage.

When it comes to handling firearms it's imperative to accept the realities of the tool. One should also consider the centuries of myths and misunderstandings concerning firearms. The big and small screens of movie theaters and television portray firearms and those who handle them in contradictory and confusing manners.

Hollywood portrays handguns as outrageously powerful tools that can send a man flying backward through a plate glass window, while in the next scene depicting characters carelessly passing pistols around with no regard to safety.

When operating a chainsaw, pouring gasoline into an engine or cooking over the blue flame of a gas range, the importance of safety stays the same. That is to demonstrate respect for the dangerous item or material that is in use. Though high explosives pose an incredible amount of danger, qualified engineers and construction workers safety use them everyday. Likewise, one can safely and effectively use a handgun as a recreational or defensive tool.

Gas and Noise

A firearm is a simple machine. It contains springs, levers and moving parts. A firearm, like most machines, needs fuel in order to function as designed. Without gasoline, a lawnmower is just a large metal object that takes up space in the garage. Without ammunition, a firearm is just an expensive paperweight.

A cartridge or round of ammunition consists of four basic components: the projectile, propellant, primer and case. Gun enthusiasts often refer to ammunition and cartridges as bullets, as the bullet leaves the barrel and travels downrange to the target, while the casing stays behind.

There is no magic or mythology involved in firing a handgun, as cartridges operate on a simple combination of science, chemistry and physics. To ignite a cartridge or round, the handgun's trigger releases the spring-loaded firing pin, the pin strikes the impact sensitive primer and the primer creates a hot spark or flame. The spark then ignites the solid propellant powder inside the cartridge case. This powder burns extremely fast and changes from a solid to a gas. The gas expands rapidly and seeks the path of least resistance through the case's mouth where the bullet sits. The gas forces the bullet at a high rate of speed into the barrel of the gun, which stabilizes the bullet for flight with its grooved rifling.

Naturally, all of those actions take place in a fraction of a second. Depending on the size of the handgun and the cartridge, the firing process may seem like a violent or shocking event. The rapid chemical change of the propellant powder from a solid to an expanding gas causes two effects for which the shooter should prepare themselves: motion and noise.

The weight of the projectile provides a certain amount of resistance when the gas pushes the projectile down the barrel. The shooter feels the resistance through their hand in what is generally referred to as recoil. Felt recoil varies tremendously based upon the volume of the powder charge and weight of the bullet. It also varies by the size, weight and construction of the firearm. As a general rule, lightweight handguns used with centerfire pistol cartridges have more felt recoil than larger, heavier handguns using similar cartridges.

Semi-automatic pistols use the burning gas and subsequent recoil from the cartridge ignition to cycle the gun's action. This can add to the overall motion of the gun in ones hands, but it can also reduce felt recoil by acting as a shock absorber.

Never shoot at an unidentified target. One should always have a clear sight of an attacker before pulling the trigger.

Eyes and Ears

As the propellant gas expands, it seeks out every possible avenue of escape. While the majority of this gas will exit the muzzle of the gun, a portion will leak out of the chamber opening and the action. This hot gas can and will force dust, lubricating oil and fragments of unburned powder or carbon to spread in all directions. While the gas from a handgun cartridge is generally not a big hazard to the skin, it can present a hazard to the shooter's eyes and the eyes of anyone in the area.

Shooters should always wear shatterproof eye protection for any type of firearm training. Wearing eye protection applies for anyone observing or nearby.

The noise generated by a cartridge firing is merely a byproduct of the expanding gas and the resistance created by the projectile. Different gun and ammunition combinations produce varied amounts of noise. They all share a common factor in hearing damage. The sharp sound produced by the gas propellant and the sometimes supersonic crack of the bullet breaking the sound barrier can and will damage the human ear.

Ringing ears indicate hearing damaged. Many people erroneously believe that after the ringing has stopped their ears return to normal, though not necessarily true. Hearing loss builds up over time and each and every gunshot can cause damage.

Shooters and spectators should always wear hearing protection when around firing weapons. Foam earplugs are better than nothing at all, though overhead protective muffs offer the best defense against hearing loss. Some even opt to wear foam earplugs and protective earmuffs when using an indoor range, as many guns fire at once. Also, when shooting at an outdoor range with an overhead cover, the noise from the gunfire will reflect from the cover back down to the shooter's ears. Double hearing protection is a wise choice in that situation as well.

Double hearing protection is best when practicing at the indoor range. That means wearing both ear plugs and overhead ear muff protectors.

Negligent or Accident

Search for the term "accidental shooting" on the Internet and the results will produce pages of news reports describing injuries and deaths associated with firearms. Let's take a serious look at the use of the term accident to see if it genuinely applies.

Law enforcement officials as a rule do not refer to vehicle crashes as accidents. People have adopted the word accident as a term to excuse or dissolve blame. When one vehicle collides with another vehicle or any object, the police refer to it as a crash or collision and not an accident, as they only seldom consider a crash inevitable. Usually a driver's negligence caused a collision.

Here's a simple example. You're driving down the street. Your cell phone buzzes and you pick it up to read a text message. As you look away from the road, you fail to see a car that has slowed to make a turn. Your car slams into the back of the other car. That incident was not an accident, but rather a product of negligence.

Similarly, the same applies to an "accidental" firearm discharge. Like a car crash, an accidental discharge typically occurs because of operator negligence. Thus, proper firearm safety and training remain essential in eliminating negligent discharges.

The Rules

Thousands of law enforcement professionals and military service people learn about gun safety through a set of four rules called the Universal Firearms Safety Rules. Years ago United States Marine Col. Jeff Cooper introduced the rules, which have become universal for good reason. These rules apply anywhere a person carries a gun and while variations of these rules exist, all convey the same basic objectives.

1 Treat **every gun** as if it is **loaded**

2 **Never allow** the **muzzle** to cover **anything** you are not willing to **destroy**

3 Keep your finger **off the trigger until** you've made the **decision to shoot**

4 **Know** your **target** and what's **beyond it**.

Rule 1: The Loaded Gun

Take a moment to closely examine the Universal Safety Rules one at a time. If you treat all guns as if they are loaded all the time, then you will handle them with respect. Never assume a firearm is unloaded. However, times arise when you need to handle a gun in an administrative fashion, such as during cleaning and maintenance. The same situation can apply when performing certain training or practice drills.

If available, it is important to have another individual inspect your firearm to ensure it is clear and safe.

For a semi-automatic pistol, the owner needs to first keep fingers straight and off the trigger. Then, remove the magazine, which is the source of ammunition. Next, lock the slide into the open position to allow the chamber to be clearly visible. You should then visually inspect the chamber and insert a finger into the chamber mouth to be sure that no cartridge remains in the chamber.

After the verification process is complete it will be safe to handle the gun for cleaning, disassembly or dry-fire practice. Despite having double-checked to make sure the gun is unloaded, you should remain conscious of the muzzle and where it is pointing.

Shooters and gun owners should always consider a handgun loaded. Always follow the same process when picking up a handgun by removing the magazine from a semi-automatic pistol and locking back the slide.

Inserting a finger into the chamber mouth is another necessary step in inspecting a gun to ensure it is unloaded.

Always remember that whenever you hold a gun that it's aimed at something. Make sure your immediate surroundings are clear and the target is visually acquired before taking aim.

Rule 2: Muzzle Direction

This rule includes the words "willing to destroy." From a practical standpoint, one cannot always hold a firearm so that it's always pointed at a target. Despite this, one should ask themselves the same question each moment they hold a firearm: Would the gun harm anyone or anything if it fired at that exact moment? If one can answer yes, then they should correct their actions and point the gun in direction where an accidental misfire couldn't harm anything. Even if one has unloaded their firearm, a middle ground doesn't exist, and one should treat all guns as a loaded gun. By not adopting this mindset, far too many people have negligently discharged a gun and injured or killed innocent bystanders.

One might ask what direction can they point a firearm when not shooting? While answers will surely vary depending upon who one asks, many experienced shooters will say one should point a gun's muzzle toward the ground at all times while not actually shooting a target. Others might say one should point their gun at the sky when not shooting.

Both answer are only partially correct.

As mentioned, a shooter must point their gun's muzzle somewhere when handling a firearm, as one can't always point their gun downrange or at the target. Those who believe one's muzzle should always face the ground assume the ground is always soft, that if a gun discharged unexpectedly the sand or grass would safely absorb the bullet and hurt no one.

The muzzle-down believers often ignore that pointing the muzzle down can mean pointing at concrete, asphalt, hard rock and brick. Should the firearm discharge in the down direction, the bullet will ricochet in an unpredictable direction or shatter and send multiple fragments of the bullet in all directions. In this scenario, the bullet or fragments could strike and harm anyone.

The opposite becomes true when discussing pointing a gun's muzzle upwards into the air. If a shooter, while outdoors, points their gun straight up and it discharges, the projectile will eventually reach terminal velocity and fall back to the earth, aided by the power of gravity. Even at this speed, a standard handgun bullet can inflict serious injury to a person.

However, a difference exists between pointing a gun directly upwards and angling the barrel upwards. A shot from a firearm held at an angle will travel under the speed of the propellant powder and may remain at a dangerous speed until it comes to rest. When shooters fire bullets into the air that ultimately kill or injure someone, often one will discover the shooter fired their gun at an angle upwards and not straight up.

Thus, circumstances usually dictates which direction one should point their muzzle when not prepared to fire. If you're checking your home for intruders on the first floor and your children are in their bedrooms on the second floor, pointing your gun up wouldn't seem like a wise choice. Conversely, if your three-year-old child clings to your leg because as a burglar attempts breaking into your house, pointing the gun down wouldn't seem like the best choice either.

Right-handed shooters should place their trigger finger so it lies along side the frame on a semi-automatic pistol when not engaged in firing.

Only put your finger on the trigger when your eyes are on the target and you have decided to fire the gun.

The trigger is not a finger rest. It is meant to fire the handgun.

The trigger finger should be placed against the cylinder when not firing with a double-action revolver.

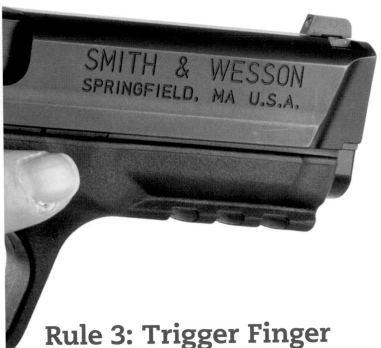

Rule 3: Trigger Finger

Shooters accidentally placing their finger on the trigger when not prepared to shoot has remained the most violated firearms safety rule over the years. In short, one should only place their finger on the trigger right before firing their weapon. If the shooter has not brought their gun into the firing position and located their target, their finger should stay off the trigger. This practice, along with never pointing a gun at an undesired target, will help prevent accidents and keep all persons around a firearm safe. Shooters shouldn't even place their fingers on the triggers of heavy double-action handguns, as these guns still prove fairly easy to fire. In the case of an emergency, a shooter can move their finger to the firing position in a fraction of a second. Thus, shooters should keep their finger above the trigger guard or below the slide area until identifying their target in their gun's sights. All shooters should routinely practice picking up and handling their weapon while not touching the trigger. Likewise, shooters should also practice finding a target in their gun's sights, moving their finger to ready position, and then firing their weapon.

Left-handed shooters should put the trigger finger on the slide and above the frame gap when not engaged in firing.

Treat all guns as a loaded gun. This practice helps further ensure an accidental discharge doesn't result in serious injury or death.

Rule 4: Know Your Target

Bullets don't always go directly where they are intended to hit. Sometimes the bullet will pass through the target and continue traveling at high velocity. That is why you must be constantly aware of what is around and beyond the target.

Experienced hunters know this rule well. A rifle bullet will often pass through the game animal and continue traveling. Far too many amateur hunters have learned a hard lesson when they shot their quarry and something else of value, a person included, was struck on the other side.

The bullet is gone at the very moment the gun is fired by the shooter. You cannot call it back. You cannot ask for a time out and try again. You are responsible for each and every shot that leaves the barrel of the gun. The shooter is ultimately responsible if the bullet strikes something or someone other than the intended target.

41

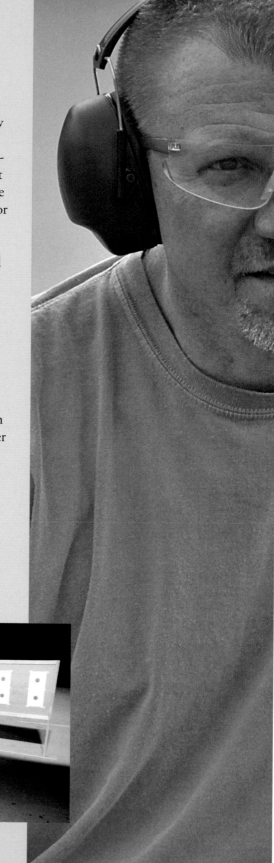

Follow the Rules

Firearms experts have reworded the Universal Safety Rules over the years, but their purpose remains the same. If you follow all four rules, the chances of inadvertently injuring a person become miniscule. Conversely, any time gunfire injures or unintentionally kills someone, you'll find the shooter violated at least one or more of the rules. As responsible citizens and shooters, we cannot simply make excuses for when a round strikes someone or something other than the target and instead must take the appropriate precautions to avoid such an accident.

When discussing unexpected firearm discharges, one should note the differences between accidental and negligent discharges. An accidental discharge occurs when the shooter or gun owner couldn't prevent the gun from going off. Though extremely rare, a gun can malfunction or component become worn or faulty, causing the gun to fire. A negligent discharge occurs when the shooter does something wrong. People get injured when the muzzle gets indexed in their general vicinity.

Because of recent news headlines and the political climate of our country, many have their eyes fixed on law-abiding gun owners. Anti-gun factions often delight each time a gun owner makes a mistake, as it gives them more fodder to debate against gun ownership.

While firearms certainly have their risks, guns would remain ineffective if they didn't have the power to neutralize a threat. Because of gun's inherent dangers, shooters and gun owners should police each other to ensure someone never unsafely uses or handles a gun. If shooters and gun owners handle their weapons with respect and care, they'll avoid harming others and give skeptics less reason to debate firearm ownership and use.

5: Cartridge Selection

Concealed carry handgun owners have many choices when choosing ammunition and one should invest time in finding the correct type for their needs. Manufacturers design clever advertising and marketing campaigns to sway uncertain buyers in their direction, which only adds to the confusion when selecting ammunition. Luckily, manufacturers now offer more and better choices than ever before. Most major manufacturers make ammunition specifically designed for self-defense use in every conventional caliber, while smaller companies also manufacture reliable ammunition, including magnum and specialty calibers.

Many of those who carry concealed weapons should consider self-defense rounds.

Advancements in quality and design have ensured that most self-defense ammunition made by reputable manufacturers works well. Manufacturers thoroughly test their ammunition and most hold their product to the same quality standards. All ammunition manufactured for law enforcement use meets or exceeds the same FBI standards with minimal differences.

Unfortunately, a magic bullet doesn't exist that any and all shooters can use. Despite this, we've provided information to supersede clever marketing campaigns so one can find the round to meet their specific needs.

Smaller calibers, such as the .22, lack the firepower to quickly drop an attacker and increase the chances of the attacker reaching you and doing harm.

Use full metal jacket or wadcutters bullets for training and practice. Hollow-point bullets are best for personal protection.

Myth Buster: Not All Ammo Works Every Time

Ammo selection begins with debunking another myth: that handguns are always effective. A concealed handgun is only marginally effective if not loaded with the proper ammunition. Handguns heavily depend on their ammunition to successfully fire and rounds tend to be somewhat unpredictable. Thus, a handgun round has limited capabilities and one cannot expect one caliber type to work well in every situation. With that, ammunition choice still remains an important factor when determining how to best defend oneself in life-threatening situations.

Larger, high energy calibers increase the likelihood of neutralizing a threat. A concealed weapon will prove ineffective and even costly if the round can't quickly penetrate an assailant's vital organs.

Myth Buster:
Bigger Is Not Always Better

Another myth involves the thought that bigger is always better. One should understand that no one caliber suits every person and every situation. Every gun "expert" has their opinion on which caliber is the best. Many conventional calibers, such as .38 special, 9mm, .40 caliber or .45 ACP, work well for some and poorly for others. Not all shooters would benefit from using the biggest, most powerful caliber, as shot placement and consistently hitting a target remains more critical. While larger or more powerful rounds generally cause more damage to a target, a shooter must effectively handle and comfortably operate their handgun.

It's critical to remember that one should use handguns in self-defense situations to stop deadly threats or serious bodily harm. If a pistol can't stop a determined criminal from doing personal harm, then it's a liability, not an asset.

Most importantly, one should choose the most powerful caliber they can handle by determining if they can accurately engage a target and make fast follow-up shots. These factors could mean the difference between stopping a lethal threat or not.

A full-sized 9mm pistol equipped with a high capacity magazine is a popular choice.

The 9mm Parabellum cartridge has been in use for over a century and remains popular for its controllability and mid-range power.

Fact: The Projectile is First

A round's projectile, or bullet, is the most effective part, as it's the only part that strikes a target. Everything else — brass, powder and primer — moves the bullet to the target.

The bullet stops a threat in one of two ways: reaching the central nervous system, spine, or brain or causing rapid blood loss. A central nervous system hit immobilizes the brain with as close to immediate incapacitation as possible. Blood loss is all about the rapid lowering of blood pressure. The heart stops after the inability to keep up with the rapid loss of blood. A bullet can cause the most rapid blood loss by puncturing holes in vital organs or arteries.

Pistol bullets are most effective when they penetrate far enough into the body and vital organs and create the largest hole possible. Well-designed self-defense bullets accomplish both results with proper shot placement. For the most part, velocity and muzzle energy determine the depth of penetration and bullet expansion determines the size of the hole.

The Best Bullet

There is no single answer to the question about which bullet is the all-around best for a pistol. The choices are many but the final selection is not so complicated. Here's why.

There are two common bullet types used in pistol ammunition. Those are full metal jacket (FMJ) and hollow point (HP). Other factors vary considerably in both categories, but these two types encompass most of the available choices. Differences in construction give the hollow point it's noticeable shape. Even so, both bullets are similar in construction and design.

Full Metal Jacket

Full metal jacket bullets are inexpensive, reliable and designed primarily for practice or target use. Most full metal jacket bullets consist of a lead core with a protective copper jacket. The jacket assists in feeding rounds and cuts down on fouling in the barrel.

The full metal jacket, as a practice bullet, typically has lower velocity than some higher powered defense rounds. Construction makes them inherently reliable in most semi-automatic firearms.

Not all handguns can fire hollow point or self-defense rounds and must instead use a full metal jacket bullet. Most military forces exclusively use full metal jacket rounds. Given that the rounds don't expand, the size and shot placement of full metal jacket rounds is imperative.

Full metal jacket bullets are inexpensive and are primarily designed for practice or targets.

Hollow-Point

Hollow-point bullets expand when entering soft tissue. Similar in design to full metal jacket ammunition, most hollow-point bullets consist of a lead core surrounded by a jacket. Gun experts usually describe hollow-points as "controlled expansion" bullets.

Most hollow-point bullets considerably expand over their initial size, one of the factors leveling the pistol caliber playing field today. Even a 9mm bullet expands to well over .50 inches with some approaching .70 inches. Comparatively, most .45 ACP rounds expand from .60 to .75 inches, making them very similar.

Various designs use petals that open and cut into tissue, or simply mushroom in size to cre-

ate larger diameters. Some hollow-points use polymer tips or other fillers to control when they expand. Recent designs include bullets made entirely of one metal.

Velocity and bullet weight determine how deep this bullet penetrates, while speed also influences how quickly the bullet expands. The ammunition industry has heavily researched and perfected this science over the years and concluded that if expansion occurs too soon, a bullet may not penetrate deep enough. The best designs open quickly while penetrating deep enough to reach vital organs.

The standard hollow-point bullet is designed for maximum expansion, making this cartridge a good choice for concealed-carry use.

Bullet Construction

The standard hollow-point bullet produces maximum expansion, making this cartridge a good choice for concealed-carry use.

Standard Hollow-Point

The standard hollow-point bullet is designed for maximum penetration, making this cartridge a good choice for concealed-carry use.

Standard hollow-point ammunition has a distinct hollowed out tip on the bullet face. This ammunition expands to maximum size when penetrating soft body tissue. The hollow-point peels back upon impact, which is sometimes known as mushrooming. This causes the bullet to slow down or stop inside the target and transfers more kinetic energy into the tissue.

Bonded Core

Manufacturers use various methods to chemically or mechanically bond the jacket to the core to prevent separation in bonded core bullets. That results in little or no separation when the bullet passes through barriers.

Construction prevents the bullet from expanding too soon or coming apart after passing through the barrier and entering the threat. Manufacturers offer bonded core bullets in many variations and designed for specific applications.

Law enforcement agencies sometimes use bonded core bullets, as they prove useful in conflicts around vehicles or behind barriers.

There is no jacket to separate with a single material bullet. This bullet is very effective for deep penetration.

Monolithic Solid

Some new bullets are constructed from a solid piece of copper, brass or other metal. There is no jacket to separate so these bullets typically stay in one piece. These bullets can be very effective with impressive expansion and deep penetration.

The one-piece construction can open up more without compromising the effectiveness of the bullet. Many seem to work well through barriers or directly into soft tissue. Large cavities can present reliability issues, so care must be taken to assure the bullet feeds into the pistol.

The design of a bonded core bullet prevents it from expanding too soon.

Ammunition Manufacturer _WILSon Combat_

Weight _230_   **Type** _XTP_   **Velocity** _865 FPS_

Bullet Accuracy

Accuracy is an important factor when choosing a self-defense bullet. Consistency is the key to accuracy. As a general rule, most factory manufactured ammunition has a similar level of accuracy, though certain guns can affect this, as certain bullets might not suit every gun.

Shot placement and accuracy are the most critical factors in stopping a threat. If a particular round simply will not shoot accurately in one's pistol, then choose another type of bullet, as one needs the best bullet for their purposes to accurately shoot. Many firearm manufacturers will have ammunition recommendations for a specific firearm and a firearm's manual may detail the ratings of ammunition for the gun.

Most factory ammunition has a high level of accuracy and generally the weapon or shooter determines accuracy.

2" x 2" Square

A solid grouping of shots is key when choosing the bullet that works best for a particular handgun.

Bullet Performance

Bullet effectiveness is important but insignificant when the bullet fails to operate in your pistol. Various hollow-point designs utilize different cavity sizes. For revolver carriers this matters little. In the semi-auto world it makes all the difference in the world.

How well the bullets feed depends on the design of the pistol, the caliber and the length of the barrel. The venerable 1911 pistol is notoriously ammunition specific when you move outside a 5-inch gun with .45 ACP ammunition. Shorter barrels are more finicky to handle. Larger hollow points are also problematic. Some pistols simply will not run some ammunition, unless fine-tuned by a competent professional gunsmith. Make certain that you thoroughly test any self-defense ammunition through a 1911 pistol prior to depending on it for your life.

Modern pistols like the Glock, Smith & Wesson M&P and others are more forgiving with bullet design and function. Design changes make them far less finicky about feeding ammunition from the magazine. While hollow-point design is less an issue, other factors can affect reliability. That makes test firing equally as important.

The shorter the pistol and slide, the more likely the gun will fail to feed hollow-point ammunition. Most designs require the bullet to jump up a feed ramp and into the chamber. Extra wide hollow points or short bullets can cause issues. Shorter slides have less inertia that require stiffer springs for proper function and altered timing. Shorter slides have less inertia that require stiffer springs for proper function and altered timing. Balancing all these factors can prove challenging.

Bullets with polymer tips and filled cavities are designed for that reason. They more closely approximate full metal jacket ammunition with improved reliability, while still operating as a hollow point.

Many of the smallest pistols shooting low velocity ammunition can be very finicky. Some will only work with certain types of ammunition. Such is the case with pistols decreasing in size and firing ammunition outside conventional calibers.

Bullets with polymer tips and filled cavities closely resemble a full metal jacket cartridge, but have better expansion and energy.

Bullet Weight

Bullet weight is another factor to consider when deciding on the proper ammo for a pistol. Bullet weight is the most often discussed and argued factor in bullet choice outside design.

There are two opposing arguments with increasing middle ground in the bullet weight debate. For self-defense use, most experts either advocate smaller bullets moving very fast, or larger bullets at moderate velocities. The logic equates to pure physics. The final word really depends on what you are carrying and how you intend to use it.

Heavier bullets maintain momentum longer to provide deeper penetration at lower velocity. They expend energy longer after entering the threat. Taken to

extreme, heavy bullets at magnum velocity can deeply penetrate a target. Though well suited for hunting, most gun owners wouldn't find these appropriate for self-defense use.

Light bullets traveling very fast occupy the other end of the debate. The .40-caliber bullet is a prime example. Some experts advocate 135-grain bullets traveling up to 1300 FPS. In theory, they expand more quickly, deliver energy faster and penetrate less. This makes them ideal for urban environments where over-penetration is a concern. Many law enforcement agencies advocate 180-grain bullets moving at approximately 1050 fps. The idea is they will continue to be effective after passing

Choose heavy bullets when penetration is the need. Otherwise, select lighter bullets for dependable accuracy and performance.

through barriers. Similarly, those using standard ammunition want increased penetration through clothing.

The best choice depends on your needs. The theory doesn't always play out in the real world and one should test various rounds in their gun. Shooters should choose heavy bullets for deep penetration or light rounds for most other uses. Such scenarios have prompted many companies to offer several choices in the middle that prove practical with any conventional caliber.

Increased effectiveness in short-barreled pistols and revolvers is another reason for lighter bullets at higher velocities. Snubby-sized revolvers can now be loaded with ammunition designated as

38+P, "P" standing for pressure.

Modern powders and lighter bullets provide more effectiveness with less muzzle flash and recoil. When looking at semi-automatics, lighter bullets can make up for lost velocity in a shorter barrel. The round experiencing the greatest advantage in recent years is the .380 ACP. Modern self-defense ammunition for this caliber adds increased velocity, safe pressures and proven bullet design.

Many concealed-carry holders using a .45 ACP pistol use 165- or 180-grain bullets in 3.5 or 3 inch barrels, instead of the standard 230-grain bullets. Improved design and overall ammunition components continue increasing the effectiveness of small pistols.

Conclusion

For self defense, one should use full metal jacket ammunition as their last choice, namely if their weapon can't cycle other rounds. Advancements in bullet design and manufacturing processes make other choices better options in self-defense scenarios.

A variation of the hollow-point bullet is a great choice, though the environment where the gun carrier will use the weapon should remain the final deciding factor. If still unsure of what ammunition type one should use, perhaps ask a local police officer or gun store employee for their recommendations.

As mentioned, choose a heavier bullet for more target penetration and a lighter bullet for less penetration. If you expect to shoot through barriers, then use a bonded or one-piece bullet, though otherwise conventional hollow points would likely serve most self-defense situations.

Test the ammo in your pistol to determine recoil and muzzle blast and make the needed changes if the rounds prove uncontrollable. Make sure you fire at least 100 rounds through your pistol to make sure it works. Trial and error offers the best match for you, the pistol and its purpose.

Use ammunition loaded by a reputable and well-known manufacturer, as this isn't the place to save money. Your life depends on how well your ammunition works, so buy the best you can afford. Mainstream manufacturers like Federal, Winchester, Remington and Hornady have proven themselves as dependable brands, though lesser known companies also make reliable ammunition.

Make a point to shoot your pistol regularly to ensure the gun and your ammunition works properly. If at all possible, don't go longer than a few months without shooting self-defense ammunition through your pistol. Don't change ammunition with every new fad. Test new products periodically, but don't change what works unless it really improves your shooting.

Taking the time to choose the best ammunition is critical. It will pay huge dividends in the long run.

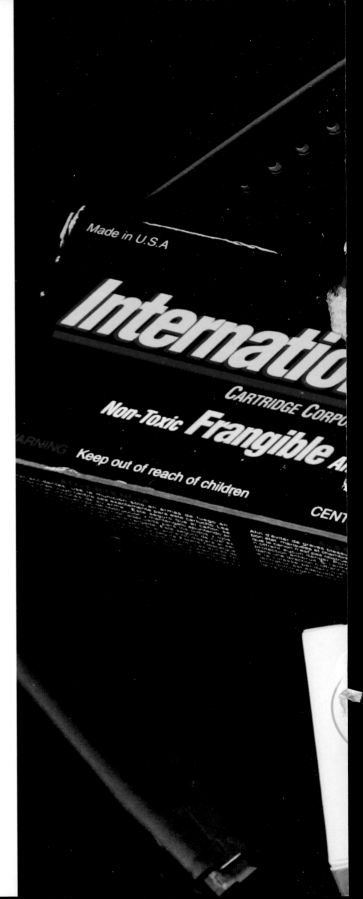

WINCHESTER®

★ ★ ★ ★ ★
★ MADE IN ★
★ USA ★
★ ★ ★ ★ ★
★ ★ ★ ★

WARNING:
Keep out of reach of children.
Read all warnings on package.

AVERTISSEMENT:
Gardez hors de la portée des enfants.
Lisez tous les avertissements sur l'emballage.

WINCHESTER®

Warning: Keep Out of Reach of Children.
Cartouches À Percussion Centrale
Mise En Garde: Gardez Hors De La Portée Des Enfants.

PISTOL & REVOLVER CARTRIDGES

50 CENT

Remington

UMC®
50 CENTERFIRE PISTOL & REVOLVER CARTRIDGES

PISTOL & REVOLVER CARTRIDGES

SAFETY RULES:

• Keep barrel clear
• Never load a gun until
• Wear eye and ear protection

REGLES DE SECURITE:

HIGH VELOCITY AMMUNITION

COR®BON

PROVEN STOPPING POWER

20 Cartridges
WARNING:
KEEP OUT REACH CHILDREN

COR®BON

6: Introduction to Semi-Automatic Pistols

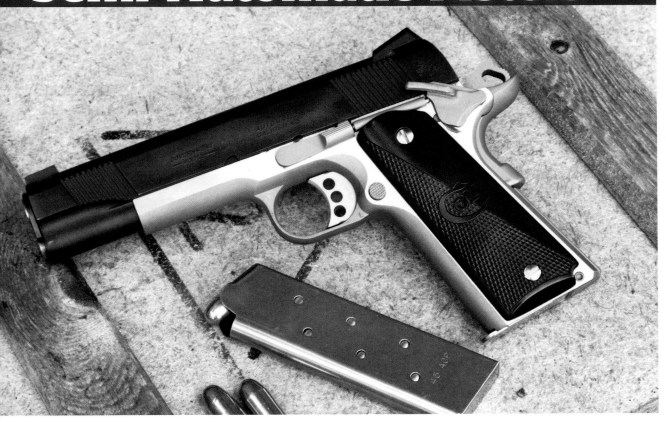

Though some debate persists, the Schönberger-Laumann Model 1892 stands as the first semi-automatic pistol to ever enter production. While historians debate over exact manufacturing dates, semi-auto pistols have remained a fixture among handgun choices for well over 100 years. No sidearm has had the same level of historical or social influence over the last two centuries as the semi-auto pistol, as soldiers have used them in every major conflict and law enforcement still carry them as their primary weapon. Most firearm enthusiasts consider the Mauser C96, Luger M1908, the Colt Models 1903 and M1911 as the forerunners to the modern pistol. When choosing a handgun to carry, one should consider semi-auto pistols as a viable option.

The guns operate on a semi-automatic mechanism, which fires a bullet, discharges a spent casing and loads a new round with every trigger pull. Unlike revolvers, which have rotating chambers, semi-auto pistols include actions that feed rounds from a magazine into the chamber after each trigger pull. Thus after each shot, the action automatically ejects a spent casing, cocks back the hammer and loads another round into place. Though revolvers can operate on double-action mechanisms that offer repeating fire, only semi-autos can self-load and extract rounds with each trigger pull.

Semi-Automatic Pistol Anatomy

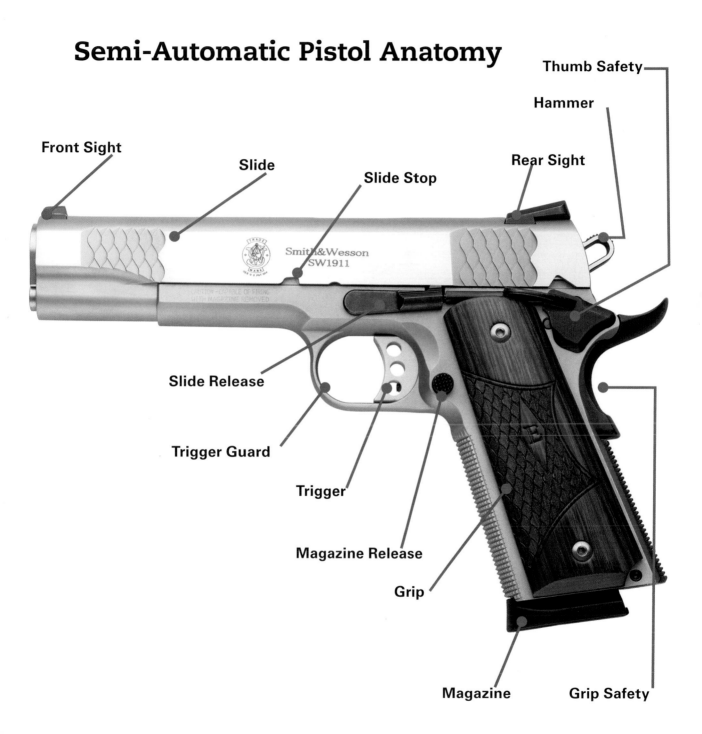

Thumb Safety

Hammer

Front Sight

Slide

Slide Stop

Rear Sight

Smith&Wesson
SW1911

Slide Release

Trigger Guard

Trigger

Magazine Release

Grip

Magazine

Grip Safety

Cycle of Operation

Self-loading guns have what manufacturers refer to as the cycle of operation. The cycle includes a series of steps, which we've listed below.

» **Feeding:** loading a fresh cartridge from the magazine
» **Locking:** the action locks or goes back into battery
» **Firing:** igniting a cartridge
» **Unlocking:** the action unlocks and begins to move
» **Extracting:** the empty case is pulled out from the chamber
» **Ejecting:** the empty case comes out and away from the gun
» **Reloading:** This stage is completed when the slide rides back forward under spring tension and pulls a fresh cartridge from the magazine and pushes it into the barrel's chamber. The slide will lock forward and the pistol is ready to fire again.

When the pistol is fired, all of the aforementioned steps or actions happen in a fraction of a second. A stoppage occurs when the cycle of operation experiences any unintentional interruption. A stoppage can occur for multiple reasons, including damaged ammunition, a dirty or fouled gun or damaged or poorly fitting parts. The shooter can also induce a stoppage by incorrectly gripping the gun.

Firing

Unlocking. Extracting. Ejecting.

Re-loading

The pistol is ready to fire again as the slide rides forward and pulls a new cartridge from the magazine into the chamber

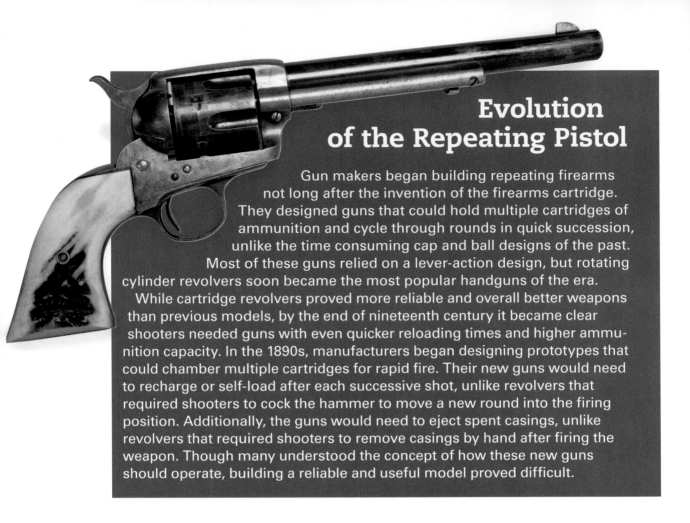

Evolution of the Repeating Pistol

Gun makers began building repeating firearms not long after the invention of the firearms cartridge. They designed guns that could hold multiple cartridges of ammunition and cycle through rounds in quick succession, unlike the time consuming cap and ball designs of the past. Most of these guns relied on a lever-action design, but rotating cylinder revolvers soon became the most popular handguns of the era. While cartridge revolvers proved more reliable and overall better weapons than previous models, by the end of nineteenth century it became clear shooters needed guns with even quicker reloading times and higher ammunition capacity. In the 1890s, manufacturers began designing prototypes that could chamber multiple cartridges for rapid fire. Their new guns would need to recharge or self-load after each successive shot, unlike revolvers that required shooters to cock the hammer to move a new round into the firing position. Additionally, the guns would need to eject spent casings, unlike revolvers that required shooters to remove casings by hand after firing the weapon. Though many understood the concept of how these new guns should operate, building a reliable and useful model proved difficult.

Semi-Auto Advantages

Semi-automatic pistols offer two primary advantages over revolvers: cartridge capacity and ease of loading and reloading. Thanks to their detachable magazines, pistols can store more rounds and offer quicker reload times, as shooters could keep spare, loaded magazines on hand to quickly insert back into the gun and continue firing. Many pistols also offer improved action and trigger designs, though a well-built 1873 Single Action Army revolver may have a lighter trigger than a modern Beretta M9 pistol. Likewise, a shooter may even find a pocket pistol more difficult to fire than a full-sized .38 Special double-action revolver.

Reloading with a full magazine of cartridges is an advantage of the semi-automatic pistol.

Common Components

Self-loading handguns share some similar features regardless of the make, model or design. Common features include a reciprocating slide or action that moves back and forth while the barrel remains relatively motionless. The motion of the slide chambers and extracts ammunition from the magazine and ejects the spent cases from the chamber.

A few older model pistols have fixed magazines that don't move or detach from the gun, but these guns are rare. The vast majority of self-loading handguns use a detachable magazine. The shooter can carry multiple, pre-loaded magazines on their person and rapidly reload the handgun after emptying each magazine.

Semi-automatic pistols with detachable magazines have a button, lever or catch that releases the magazine from the gun, though these releases vary depending on each gun's design. Other common components include some type of grip frame used to hold and control the pistol.

The Safety

Most modern firearms have numerous built-in safety mechanisms. The shooter manually operates and engages some of these mechanisms, but others are internal and passive, operating without the shooter's aid.

Over the years, lever or button-operated safeties have remained both popular and useful. Guns with lever or button safeties typically have them attached to the side of the frame or to the rear of the slide. Shooters either press down or push forward on the lever to disengage the safety, though this varies between models. Many safety levers also function as de-cocking mechanisms.

Manufacturers also use grip safeties on many semi-automatic pistols. Guns with grip safeties usually have a pad or lever on the back of the grip that the shooter must engage before firing the gun. The safety relies on the shooter applying a certain amount of pressure to the grip or pad to disengage the safety.

As for internal or passive safeties, most modern firearms have a drop safe or firing pin block. This prevents the gun from discharging if accidentally dropped or struck by a hard blow. A hammer block safety functions in a

similar fashion. Only after the shooter presses the trigger will the hammer-block safety disengage and allow the gun to fire.

Depending on the make and model, a pistol may have a magazine disconnect safety. This device prevents the gun from firing unless the detachable magazine is fully seated into the gun. While this would seem an excellent addition, some magazine disconnect safeties negatively affect a gun's trigger press, making it heavier and more difficult to depress smoothly.

Some guns include key lock safeties, which require the shooter to insert a specially designed key into a locking mechanism before firing the weapon. Key lock safeties ensure those without the special key cannot use the gun.

Here's a note of caution: many versions of key lock safeties malfunction after the lock's tiny components succumbed to the gun's repeated recoil. Shooters have also needed to use their gun, but forgot they'd locked their gun and thus couldn't shoot. Those in life threatening situations could find the latter situation particularly troubling.

Most shooters would consider a mechanical safety, particularly a firing pin or hammer block, a prudent addition to any design. The trouble comes when someone attempts to substitute mechanical safeties for safe gun handling.

As mentioned previously, gun owners and shooters can best avoid misfires and accidental shootings by handling their weapon with care and attentiveness. Those using or around those with a gun have the responsibility to guarantee a situation remains safe. A mechanical safety can never act as a substitute to wise and responsible thinking.

The Beretta M9 (Model 92) uses a traditional double-action trigger and de-cock/ safety lever on the slide.

The 1911 pistol uses both a manual
safety lever, found on the frame, and a
grip safety in the backstrap.

Handgun Actions

One could simply describe a firearm's action as the group of moving parts that control the firing and operation of the gun. In the most simplistic terms, every firearm has three basic part groups: the barrel, grip and action. The action consists of the trigger, hammer, springs, levers and the other mechanical components.

When shopping for a handgun, one will likely hear the term 'action' thrown around somewhat vaguely. Most experts in the field simply use the word to describe how a weapon functions. Action relates to the following terms.

» Double-Action
» Single-Action
» Double-Action/Single-Action
» Double-Action Only
» Striker-Fired

While some would include a few more descriptors, the above list includes the most prevalent.

With so many terms, a new shooter could easily think double-action means a gun can shoot two ways. Likewise, one could easily think single-action means a gun only shoots one way. A simple way distinguish the two is to determine how many jobs the trigger accomplishes when pulled. If the trigger only releases a pre-cocked hammer or firing pin, the gun is single-action. If the trigger brings back the hammer and then releases it to fire, the gun is double-action.

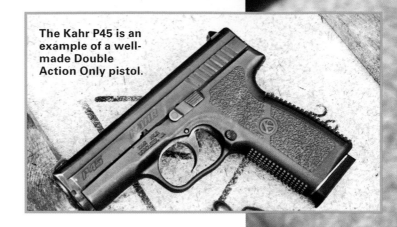

The Kahr P45 is an example of a well-made Double Action Only pistol.

Striker fired pistols fire with an internal striker or firing pin housed inside the slide. When the slide opens, it partially cocks the spring-loaded striker. When the shooter presses the trigger, they complete the final portion of the cocking process and release the striker.

The advantage of a striker-fired pistol is a single and consistent trigger press for the shooter. Also, from a practical standpoint, the shooter doesn't have to cock the striker as they do with a traditional single-action revolver and instead the trigger completes the cocking and firing process.

Single-action pistols date back to the origination of the self-loading handgun, while manufacturers introduced double-action pistols in the 1930s. Double-action handguns experienced widespread popularity in the U.S. during the 1970s and 1980s. Striker-fired pistols have dominated handgun designs in the 21st century as have the new breed of very smooth double-action only pistols.

Springfield Armory's XD(M) pistol is a striker-fired gun with many attractive features.

Semiautomatic handguns provide shooters a distinct advantage in various scenarios with their high capacity magazines, ease of use and broad availability.

Modern Semi-Autos

Modern examples of self-loading handguns include the Beretta M9, a traditional double-action pistol. The first trigger pull is long and heavy, given the gun's double-action mechanisms. After the first trigger pull, the shooter will find successive shots shorter and lighter. Additionally, the gun features a de-cocker/safety on its slide.

The SIG Sauer P226 stands as another standard, quality double-action pistol. Unlike the Beretta with its safety/de-cocking lever, the P226 has a de-cocking lever on the left side of the frame and no manual safety lever.

The Colt Model 1911 and its subsequent variations and replicas remain, as mentioned, the most noted traditional single-action pistol ever produced. The 1911 features an exposed hammer that stays cocked after the shooter chambers a round. This pistol has a manual thumb safety lever attached to the frame and a grip safety mechanism on the back of the frame.

Striker-fired guns include the Glocks, Smith & Wesson M&Ps and some Rugers. While each of these handguns has unique characteristics, for all practical purposes they function the same. Because of their multiple internal safeties, Glock or Smith & Wesson M&P pistols don't need external safeties and these brands have thus proven themselves as some of the safest guns available.

Several manufacturers produce smooth and manageable double-action only or DAO pistols, Kahr Arms and Kel-Tec among these with quality DAO triggers. Kahr's patented DAO trigger is one of the best available, although both companies make DAO pistols that feature few external controls other than the trigger, magazine release button and the slide-lock. The guns don't use manual safeties or de-cocking levers.

The de-cock lever is on the left side of the SIG P226 DA/SA pistol.

Kahr Arm's patented DAO trigger is coveted for its smooth press.

Manual of Arms

In military lingo "manual of arms" refers to the approved method for operating a particular gun. Many new shooters shy away from a self-loading pistol because of all the moving parts, buttons, latches and levers. To the new gun owner, a pistol with de-cocking levers and manual safeties can seem daunting.

During the next few paragraphs you will learn more about the most practical and efficient manual of arms for the self-loading pistol. We'll base our examples off the Glock Model 17 9x19mm.

Glock 17: Manual of Arms

Hold the pistol in your dominant hand. Using your support side hand, retrieve a loaded magazine. Placing your support hand index finger down the side of the magazine will aid with insertion.

With elbows tucked against the ribcage and gun pointed toward target, insert a magazine into the well of the pistol. Seat the magazine firmly with the palm of the support hand. Resist the urge to tap the magazine base. One should not need to force the magazine into the pistol. If the magazine will not seat without being forced, remove one round of ammunition.

With the magazine fully inserted and properly seated, bring the support hand up and over the top of the pistol. Grasp the rear portion of the slide. Deliberately move the hand from base of the gun directly up the side of the firearm. Doing so prevents the negligent action of placing the support hand in front of the muzzle.

Almost every self-loading pistol has some type of gripping serrations positioned at the upper rear portion of the slide. This is by design to provide a rough surface for grasping the grip. At the same time, draw the slide of the pistol to the rear with the support hand. Do so while pushing the grip and frame forward with the dominant hand. This provides a push-and-pull action that aids the shooter in fully cycling the slide.

When the slide reaches maximum rearward travel distance, release it immediately. That allows the internal recoil spring to drive the slide forward and lock the action. Resist the desire to ride the slide forward with the support hand. Allowing the support hand to ride the slide forward has historically been one of several ways that a shooter can induce a stoppage in the pistol. The recoil spring and slide can withstand the recoil inertia from a live round and thus tough enough to undergo the minimal pressure of charging the weapon.

After the slide closes, move the support hand down the side of the pistol and join it with your strong hand. Or, holster the pistol if not intended for use. Regardless of which action is taken, a shooter should ensure their trigger finger remains straight and along the slide area. One shouldn't put their finger on the trigger until prepared to fire.

The manual of arms for other types of self-loading handguns varies based upon the manufacturer's specifics. However, drawing the slide briskly to the rear and releasing it is a worthwhile skill to master with a semi-automatic pistol.

The Glock 17 in caliber 9X19 is the most widely used law enforcement pistol in the world. It offers an above-average magazine capacity of 17 cartridges.

Pistols can be fired with one hand but are more effective when both are used to grip the gun.

 Manufacturers have developed a plethora of options for semiautomatic pistols. Nearly every shooter can take advantage of the multiple sizes, grips, sights and action types available to perfectly fit his or her needs.

Running the Semi-Automatic Pistol

All firearms have similarities and unique handling characteristics. In order to effectively and efficiently make use of a semi-automatic handgun, the shooter needs to take into account several features that make self-loading pistols unique.

A shooter can operate a pistol with a single hand, but most will find controlling and accurately shooting a gun easier with both hands wrapped around the grip. When grasping a pistol, ensure the strong hand holds the gun high up on the the back-strap, the deep seat or curve at the top rear of the grip. You want to fill in that gap without reaching over it and the shooter will experience greater control when pressing the trigger and holding the gun during recoil.

Then you should take the strong hand and wrap it firmly around the grip to secure the weapon. Think of this as giving someone a firm and confident handshake. Don't try and crush the grip, but also don't hold it so loosely that it may fall out of your hand.

After holding the gun with the strongest hand, you should wrap the supporting hand around the strong and dominant hand. Think of it again like giving yourself a firm handshake. Both thumbs should touch each other on the same side of the frame, or what many shooters call stacking your thumbs. Both thumbs should be pointed downrange in the direction of the target.

Novice shooters have a tendency to cross their thumbs, but this weakens the grip and puts the top thumb in a bad position behind the slide. When the slide drives backward during recoil, the rails may contact the crossed thumb and cause injury, though most find this stinging injury more embarrassing than painful. Thus, shooters should keep both hands on the grip and stack their thumbs while shooting their semi-automatic pistol.

Shooters should also avoid the desire to cup the support hand under the bottom of the pistol, as it weakens the grip and provides little support during recoil. Keep in mind the idea is to make the most contact with the pistol grip and frame as possible, as the more contact made with the frame, the easier you can steady the pistol for accurate shooting.

Poor or limp grips often lead to stoppage when using relatively light, compact pistols. The gun needs to have some pressure on the grip to cycle properly during recoil.

One should ensure they place the trigger finger on the trigger's face the same way each time they fire their weapon. For a semi-automatic pistol, place the pad of the trigger finger on the face of the trigger and press it smoothly and deliberately. Semi-automatic pistols feature a mechanical trigger reset, which allows the shooter to quickly fire again. With that, the shooter must allow the trigger to move forward enough after each shot so the mechanical reset can engage.

Learning to shoot a pistol in consistent fashion with accuracy requires spending time getting used to the feel of the trigger. Constantly removing the finger from the trigger after each shot increases the learning curve when it comes to running the trigger.

Troubleshooting

Despite the fact shooters have numerous semi-automatic handguns from which to choose, you can learn to operate the self-loading pistol in a judicious and efficient manner with most pistols. Dealing with stoppage is a prime example, as one can apply a few simple steps when dealing with almost any pistol that has a reciprocating slide and detachable magazine. One of the most common stoppages is failure to fire, in which the shooter pulls the trigger and the gun clicks instead of discharging. Failure to fire usually occurs because the shooter has failed to chamber a round. In some cases, failure to fire is caused by a bad cartridge primer. When a failure to fire occurs, the shooter should loosen their support hand and briskly tap the magazine to ensure it hasn't come unseated. If the magazine has remained seated, the shooter should pull back the slide and let the recoil spring drive the slide home. In most cases, this will fix the stoppage and the gun will again fire. Experienced shooters call this process the tap-rack drill.

Another common stoppage or interruption in the cycle is a feed-way obstruction. This obstruction involves a spent brass casing or empty cartridge not ejecting and catching in the slide before it could eject. Like a failure to fire, one should follow the tap-rack drill to clear the gun.

While less frequent, the last typical semi-automatic pistol stoppage is a double-feed. This stoppage occurs when the gun tries to work both a live piece of ammunition and a spent casing into the chamber or the gun tries to feed two live cartridges into the chamber. Unfortunately, the tap-rack drill will not fix this problem and requires the shooter to lock the slide to the rear using the slide latch. This relieves the recoil spring tension. After this, you should remove the magazine, which will often cause cartridges or cases to fall out. For good measure, you should cycle the slide several times and retrieve a fresh magazine if possible.

You might discover during the tap-rack drill the slide locked to the rear on an empty magazine. This is a quick fix. Press the magazine release button or latch. Then drop the empty magazine away. Replace it with a loaded magazine then rack the slide with your support hand and carry on.

As you can see from the previous paragraphs, learning to master a very simple, but important manual of arms offers numerous benefits. By knowing these steps, one can properly load their weapon and rapidly and effectively clear stoppages.

If the target is paper, cardboard or steel then quickly fixing a stop doesn't matter much, but this changes if the target is bent on harming you and can shoot back. The faster you fix a stoppage, the greater chance you have of defending yourself against a threat.

A stovepipe occurs when a piece of brass becomes trapped during the cycling process. Clear the stoppage with a tap-rack drill.

If the magazine comes unseated a fresh round will fail to feed.

The double-feed stoppage occurs when two objects attempt to occupy the same space.

CAUTION-CAPABL

Crimson Trace

Read all warnin

Semi-Auto Recap

There is nothing new, mysterious or extra-deadly about a semi-automatic or self-loading handgun, despite how the news or certain movies portray them. The gun's basic design is more than a century old and, though they deserve respect, one should have every right to own and use these tools. Like any other machine, such as a motorcycle or automobile, the more you familiarize yourself with your gun, the more effectively and safely you can use them. As experts in the field often say, you should "run your machine" to feel comfortable using it.

7: Revolvers for Self Defense

Civilians have used revolvers for self-defense protection for decades and the guns remain a viable choice for concealed carry today. Law enforcement officers carried revolvers as their primary gun long before the advent of the semi-automatic pistol. Given their reliability, revolvers remain a popular and logical choice for a concealed carry weapon and many law enforcement still rely on them today as their backup weapon. While no gun is foolproof, some revolver enthusiasts believe that the fewer parts in a revolver make them prone to jamming less than semi-automatic pistols, when a jam could jeopardize one's chance of survival.

Since their introduction, revolvers have gone through continuous design refinements and enhanced modifications. Manufacturers have improved revolvers' accuracy and reliability, reduced their size and lightened their weight, making them good choices for concealed carry. Modern materials and high-tech machining have also kept them competitively priced and widely available in the marketplace. While certainly not for everyone, many will find revolvers well suited for self-defense applications, but one should invest some time and thought to determine if a revolver is best for them.

Revolver Anatomy

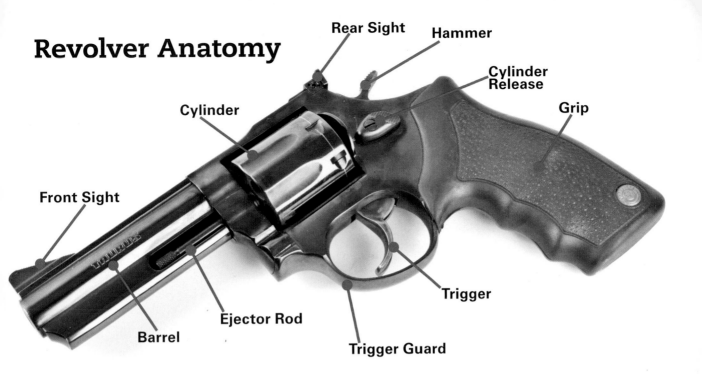

Rear Sight

Hammer

Cylinder Release

Grip

Cylinder

Front Sight

Trigger

Ejector Rod

Barrel

Trigger Guard

Revolver Choices

Revolvers cover the entire spectrum of available calibers, sizes and configurations. Manufacturers categorize their frames by small, medium and large sizes. Manufacturers typically designate frame size with a letter such as the "J-frame."

Most shooters use large frame revolvers and powerful cartridges for hunting or long-range shooting. Additionally, many of these large frame revolvers feature various sized barrels.

Medium frame revolvers, available in various barrel lengths, have been popular with police officers and security professionals. The .357 Magnum is a common caliber for medium frame revolvers.

Many who carry a small frame revolver commonly wear them on a holster or carry them inside a purse, bag or pocket. Available barrel lengths typically range from 1 to 3 inches. Many small frame revolvers chamber the .38 Special, though available in a wide range of calibers.

Revolvers played a key role in the early development of modern firearms. From the days of Wyatt Earp to today's modern police units, the revolver remains a popular and reliable choice.

Self-Defense Options

When selecting a revolver, one should first define their self-defense needs and where they anticipate using their weapon. Or more specifically, does one plan on taking their gun in public or leaving it at home in case of intruders? While carry permit holders need a reliable, forceful gun to neutralize a threat in both situations, various types of revolvers can differently serve these two locations.

To protect the home, one should keep their weapon in a safe, drawer, cabinet or anywhere they can quickly access the gun in the event of an unwanted intruder. One should also ensure the gun they keep at home stays out of the hands of children and those who may use the gun irresponsibly. For concealed carry, many choose to carry smaller, more compact revolvers, but for home defense one may feel freer to use larger framed or larger caliber revolvers. With that, while some may find larger caliber revolvers well suited for home defense, keep in mind these large caliber revolvers have more energy. This increased energy is good for stopping a threat, but can also travel through more walls and potentially harm those on the other side. Large caliber revolvers would work well in a home defense scenario for those who live in the country or away from people, as they have to worry less about stray bullets harming innocent bystanders and stand a greater chance of neutralizing a threat.

Home invasions can occur at night just as they can during the day and make weapon mounted lights and aiming devices (like lasers or red dots) a practical addition to some revolvers or handguns. These optional features added to a revolver could help a shooter identify a target or intruder in the dark and thus take a more accurate, reliable shot.

Carrying a revolver on your person presents a different set of circumstances due to the gun's size. Weight is critical because some may find heavy pistols uncomfortable to carry over extended periods of time. Additionally, long barrels make concealment a challenge.

While revolvers have their challenges — namely their size — some will find their ease of use and reliability perfect for their needs and environment. Before purchasing a revolver, perhaps borrow one from a friend or rent one from a local shooting range or gun shop to evaluate if a revolver — large or small — would suit your needs.

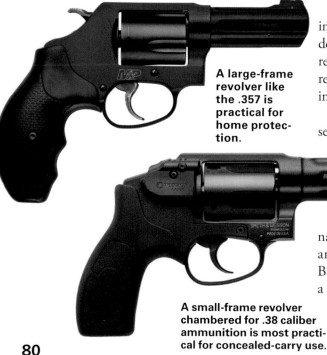

Carrying a revolver on your person presents a different set of circumstances due to the gun's size.

A large-frame revolver like the .357 is practical for home protection.

A small-frame revolver chambered for .38 caliber ammunition is most practical for concealed-carry use.

The ability to mount lights on rails below the barrel is another advantage of revolvers.

Lights On

Revolvers have the ability to mount lights on rails below the barrel. While somewhat controversial, weapon-mounted lights could prove life-saving if properly used. These options allow you to keep both hands on the grip and clearly identify the perceived threat. Such pinpoint identification is critical in a household environment.

Revolver Barrels

When purchasing a pistol, a shooter should choose a barrel length that best supports their concealment and firepower needs. Longer barrels are generally more controllable and provide higher velocities. Magnum calibers often need these longer barrels, at least 4-6-inches, to perform properly, while hunters and target shooters typically use 8-inch or longer barrels for accurate shooting. Longer barrels have a longer sight radius, making it easier to shoot more precisely, but often carrying a weapon in public requires compromise regarding barrel length.

Revolvers with 4- to 6-inch barrels have remained the most common choice for those carrying revolvers for duty or security work, as they provide a good mix of accuracy, control and weight. Most revolver manufacturers produce nearly all of their calibers in a wide variety of barrel lengths. A revolver chambered for .357 Magnum caliber with a 4- or 6-inch barrel makes a good choice for duty use, however, some may find these barrels difficult for concealed carry.

Snub-nosed revolvers feature barrels less than three inches long. These shorter barrels, which can somewhat compromise velocity, often prove the easiest to conceal and carry in public. Again, while longer barrels often provide more velocity and better accommodate larger rounds, many will find snub-nosed guns the best option to carry in public, as they fit well within a pocket, purse or discrete holster. The .38+P (high-pressure) load is a popular, easy-to-use snub-nose round.

Most shooters will find high pressure loads controllable. The 38+P (high pressure) load is reliable and easy to use.

Large vs. Small Revolver Calibers

The average concealed carrier will find revolvers chambered for .38 Special controllable, while experienced shooters might feel larger caliber and magnum loads better fit their needs.

Large caliber rounds — such as .44 Special and .45 ACP rounds — are viable for concealed carry within reason and, as mentioned, are often good for home defense. Proper handling and shooting with high power revolvers takes practice and a willingness to deal with their punishing recoil. Anything larger than a .44 Special or .45 ACP round is probably not for most concealed carry permit holders. Though some experienced marksmen choose to use extremely high powered rounds when hunting, we wouldn't recommended carrying guns of these calibers in public, as most will find them difficult to control. Most should to stick to standard caliber rounds when choosing a gun to carry concealed.

Most .357 Magnum revolvers can also chamber .38 Special rounds, which makes the gun versatile and another good caliber to potentially carry as a concealed weapon. Calibers smaller than a .38 caliber often lack the firepower to stop an assailant and thus neutralize a threat, making them not ideal to use as a self-defense round.

Single-Action Revolvers

Single-action revolvers require cocking the hammer to make the gun fire. Double-action revolvers work differently. They shoot when the trigger is pressed to make the hammer cock and then fire, or you can cock it single-action style.

Single-action revolvers are excellent weapons for home defense if you know how to use them. Reloading is slower unless you are skilled with this gun, but they should not be discounted for those who use them all the time.

Single-action revolvers are popular in a sport called Cowboy Action Shooting. It's a type of three-gun match utilizing a combination of pistol, rifle and shotgun. The hobby is popular with reenactors of cowboy western lore.

Revolvers chambered for .44 Special are controllable by the average concealed carry holder.

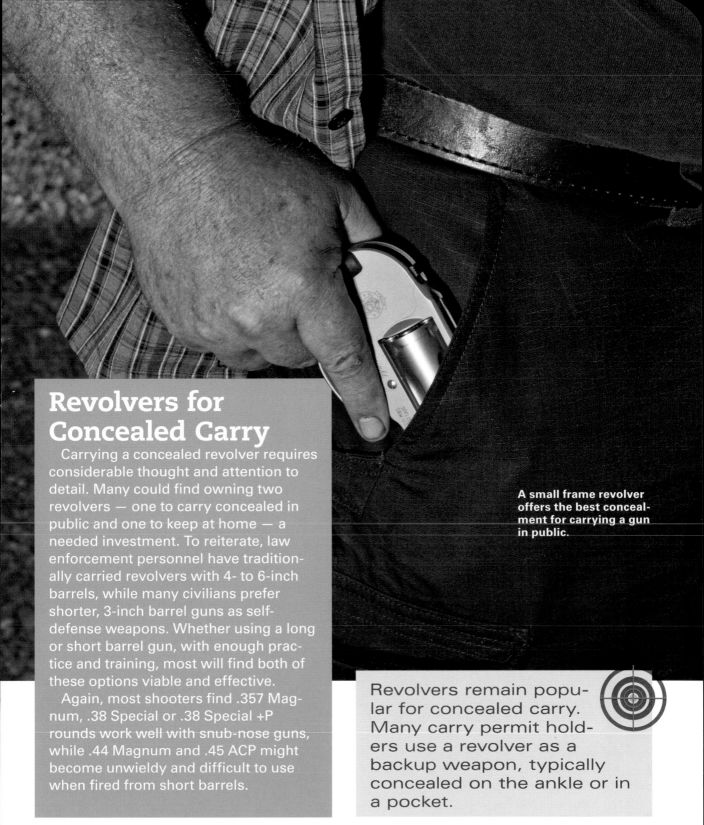

Revolvers for Concealed Carry

Carrying a concealed revolver requires considerable thought and attention to detail. Many could find owning two revolvers — one to carry concealed in public and one to keep at home — a needed investment. To reiterate, law enforcement personnel have traditionally carried revolvers with 4- to 6-inch barrels, while many civilians prefer shorter, 3-inch barrel guns as self-defense weapons. Whether using a long or short barrel gun, with enough practice and training, most will find both of these options viable and effective.

Again, most shooters find .357 Magnum, .38 Special or .38 Special +P rounds work well with snub-nose guns, while .44 Magnum and .45 ACP might become unwieldy and difficult to use when fired from short barrels.

A small frame revolver offers the best concealment for carrying a gun in public.

Revolvers remain popular for concealed carry. Many carry permit holders use a revolver as a backup weapon, typically concealed on the ankle or in a pocket.

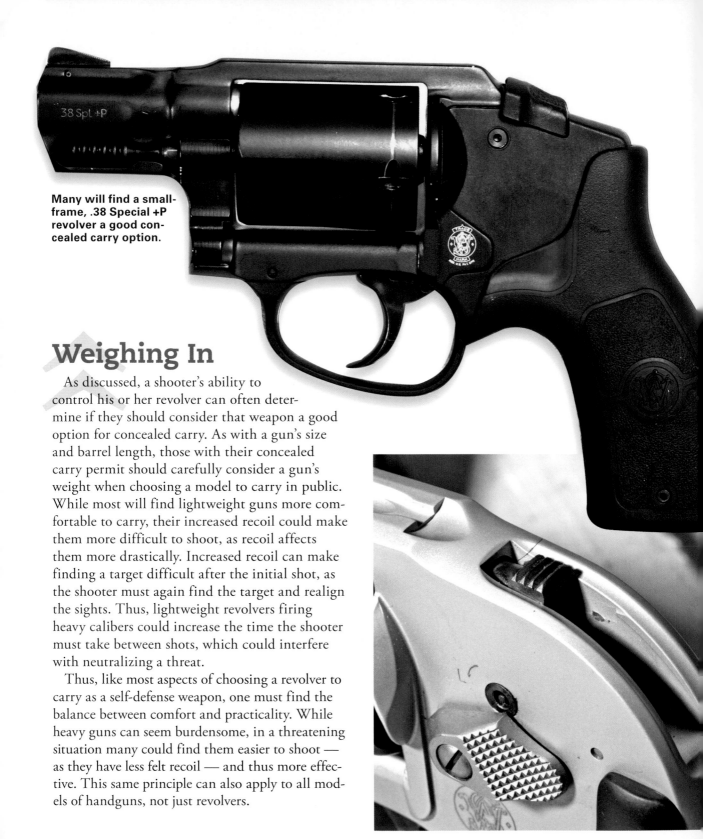

Many will find a small-frame, .38 Special +P revolver a good concealed carry option.

Weighing In

As discussed, a shooter's ability to control his or her revolver can often determine if they should consider that weapon a good option for concealed carry. As with a gun's size and barrel length, those with their concealed carry permit should carefully consider a gun's weight when choosing a model to carry in public. While most will find lightweight guns more comfortable to carry, their increased recoil could make them more difficult to shoot, as recoil affects them more drastically. Increased recoil can make finding a target difficult after the initial shot, as the shooter must again find the target and realign the sights. Thus, lightweight revolvers firing heavy calibers could increase the time the shooter must take between shots, which could interfere with neutralizing a threat.

Thus, like most aspects of choosing a revolver to carry as a self-defense weapon, one must find the balance between comfort and practicality. While heavy guns can seem burdensome, in a threatening situation many could find them easier to shoot — as they have less felt recoil — and thus more effective. This same principle can also apply to all models of handguns, not just revolvers.

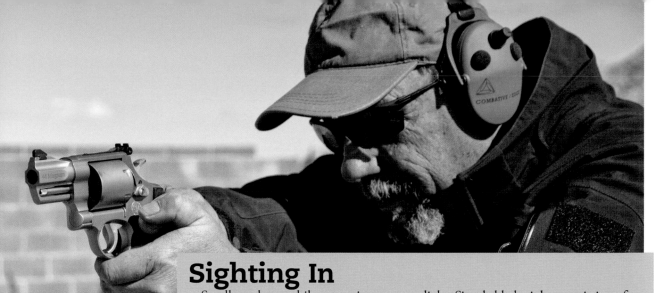

Sighting In

Small revolvers, while convenient to carry, are usually less accurate at anything further than close range. However, gun sights are improving with technology and design enhancements. The distance between the front and rear sight is called the sight radius. A longer sight radius often provides a better sight picture and helps better align the gun to the target. Shooters will usually find shorter pistols less accurate for this reason.

Sights that glow in the dark are also helpful. Larger fiber optic sights have become popular, as they make targets easy to see in bright sunlight or in low light. Simple blade sights consisting of a groove in the top of the pistol and a bump at the end are the least usable and require the shooter stay close to the target to accurately shoot. This shortcoming has made the addition of grip or integrated lasers a viable option for small revolvers, as they are typically affordable, reliable, and shooter friendly.

Though a useful tool, make sure you practice with and without laser sights, as batteries can fail in trying situations. Again, because electronically controlled devices have their risks, ensure you can shoot well with and without them.

Exposed Hammers

Another option available for revolvers is the exposed hammer. Most revolvers have a hammer that the shooter can see and use his or her thumb to cock. With that, some newer model revolvers feature partially or fully covered hammers.

Exposed hammers allow the shooter to cock the revolver and use it in single-action mode. As a single-action, the trigger requires less pressure to pull back and fire, which can assist accuracy. Despite this, some feel that manually cocking a hammer wastes valuable time in life-threatening situations and emergencies.

Exposed hammers can also hook and snag on objects in a pocket or purse, which makes them risky when it comes time to draw the gun. In those cases, an enclosed or shrouded hammer is the best option, as it allows shooters to more easily access their gun without interfering with its components.

Enclosed hammer revolvers are also ideal for ankle carry, where hooking on things and accumulating dirt is typically an issue. As a rule, medium-sized or larger revolvers come with an exposed hammer, while small revolvers often have partially or completely covered hammers.

Revolver Concealment

Concealing and carrying a revolver is similar to carrying any other gun. Those who carry small revolvers typically carry them on their hip or inside or outside their waistband. Many may find medium and large frame revolvers better suited to carry outside of a waistband, but in either case we'd recommend a quality holster.

Revolvers tend to sit higher above the waistband, adding additional weight which can make them top heavy and may require wearing a stiff belt. This same characteristic makes them well suited for cross-draw carry, which is convenient for carrying while driving a vehicle.

Revolvers are ideal for ankle carry and equally comfortable when wearing a shoulder rig. While most will find revolvers too large to carry inside a pocket, many work well for bringing along in purses, bags and cases.

The lack of a mechanical safety and double-action feature makes many revolvers quick to access and safe when rolling around in a handbag.

Some new to carrying concealed weapons may prefer a semi-automatic pistol over a revolver, as they have higher ammo capacities, typically lighter trigger pull and often available in a more compact size. Despite this, new shooters shouldn't discount revolvers, as with enough practice, almost any gun could help defend oneself against an attack.

But ultimately, regardless of barrel length, size or weight, a new shooter or those deciding to carry a concealed weapon should pick a weapon they'll actually feel comfortable carrying in public. If a gun has all the practicality in the world, fires large rounds and has proven itself reliable, but its owner doesn't carry it because they find it uncomfortable, then the gun is ultimately useless. Considering this, while a .44 Magnum might neutralize a threat better than other rounds, if the shooter finds the gun uncomfortable and often leaves it at home, we'd argue a smaller, more comfortable gun as a much better choice. In essence, carrying and having a gun — regardless of make or model — is better than finding oneself in a life-threatening situation with no gun at all.

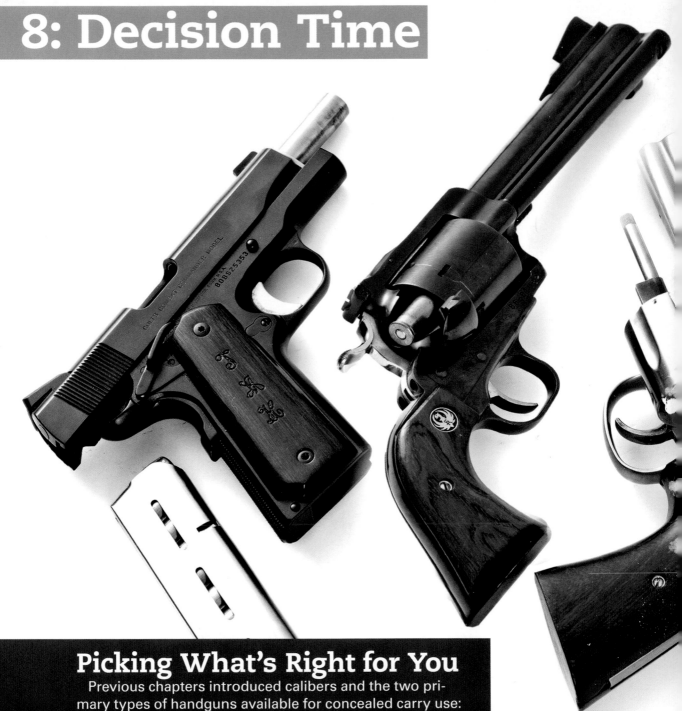

Picking What's Right for You

Previous chapters introduced calibers and the two primary types of handguns available for concealed carry use: semi-automatics and revolvers. This chapter takes into further account the available options for revolvers and semi-automatic pistols so you can continue evaluating which handgun would best fit your needs and deter an attack.

Semi-automatic pistols and revolvers (left to right). Colt Commander .45 ACP, Ruger .44 Mag. Single Action revolver, Smith & Wesson 686 .357 Magnum Double-Action revolver.

Getting Started

Unfortunately there is no universal handgun that works perfectly for everyone. In the same sense, not every caliber is a perfect selection.

It would be ideal to walk into a gun shop and announce, "I'm a size five, and I'll take that in a magnum." Unfortunately it won't be simple deciding which gun is right for you, but it can be made easier. Picking out the right handgun and caliber combination isn't as difficult when you take a methodical, well thought-out approach. Here's how to begin.

The first part of making a decision takes some effort, but there is no cost involved other than a pencil and a pad of paper. Even if you have never been exposed to firearms, don't worry. Take a few moments to list exactly how you plan to use your new handgun.

Ask yourself the following questions. Will the handgun stay at home? Do you plan to use it as a concealed weapon when you're away from home? Are you the sole user or will it be shared with family members? Will the handgun be used for recreation, self-defense or both?

This is the time to take a serious and honest approach. Think about your health, strength and the amount of time you are willing to dedicate to practice. These points should be noted in the list.

Before you wrap up this process, add a note for yourself. At the bottom of the list, write down whether or not you have a driver's license. This is a reminder that if you can drive a car then you can learn to handle a handgun. The handgun is much smaller, easier to operate and safer.

The task of learning how to safely operate a handgun may seem daunting, but think back to when you first learned how to drive. It's now second nature, and the same theory applies to handguns.

Make a list of practical needs and uses for the environment where you will carry a concealed handgun. Then seek out reputable gun dealers in your area for advice and selection of what gun is best for you.

Single-Action Revolver

The next step is to review the choices on the type of handgun actions mentioned in previous chapters. If you have ever seen a cowboy or western movie, you have seen the revolvers they used during that time period. Fully functional replicas are made today and are often thought of as the most beautiful handguns available.

While revolvers are some of the easiest handguns to operate, there are pros and cons.

Most single-action revolvers operate by opening a small loading gate on the side. Once open, a cartridge is inserted as the cylinder is rotated by hand. The process is repeated until all of the rounds are loaded and the gate is closed. Normally you have six available shots. Once all shots are fired, it comes time to eject the empty cases and load again. When reloaded, if you pulled the trigger nothing would happen. A single-action revolver requires the hammer to be cocked for every shot. With most firearms it takes little physical force to cock the hammer back. Once cocked, it also takes some physical force to pull the trigger.

What may be easy while you are practicing at a handgun range may cause problems when you are under the stress of trying to save your life. Adrenaline can affect your shooting. There are several documented cases of people with a single-action handgun constantly pulling the trigger while forgetting to cock the hammer. In this time of stress, they couldn't understand why the gun didn't fire.

The last point to look at is the process of lowering the hammer without firing. This happens if the weapon is cocked and you decide not to pull the trigger. It requires carefully lowering the hammer and easing it down while pulling the trigger. The majority of accidental discharges take place when the hammer is dropped too quickly. Special care should be taken to assure the gun muzzle is pointed in a safe direction.

The Single-Action revolver requires loading and unloading one cartridge at a time, which makes it an unwise choice for a primary concealed-carry gun.

Purchase a quality handgun. Your life may depend on this gun, so don't skimp on a cheaply made weapon.

Double-Action Revolver

The next choice is a double-action revolver. Double-action revolvers also have pros and cons that need to be addressed before deciding if this style of revolver is right for you. Typically, the entire cylinder swings out to expose the empty chambers that can be loaded one or two at a time. You can also load the gun all at once with a speed loader.

Double-action means there are two methods of firing the gun. You can cock the hammer and fire, or the hammer cocks for you when you press the trigger. The first method is called single-action mode and the second method is called double-action. Firing in double-action requires more force with a longer trigger pull than using the single-action mode.

Use safety precautions should you have the hammer cocked and decide not to fire. This requires easing down the hammer while keeping the gun pointed in a safe direction.

The double-action revolver like the Smith & Wesson 686 is a reliable choice for concealed-carry use. This revolver is chambered for .357 Magnum.

The semi-automatic Colt Commander in .45 ACP makes an ideal concealed-carry gun. It is a magazine-fed recoil-operated handgun.

Semi-Automatic Pistol

A semi-automatic pistol is another popular option for concealed carry holders. Revolvers use a cylinder to hold the cartridges. Semi-automatic pistols use magazines to hold the cartridges. The magazine is loaded outside of the gun. Then, the magazine is inserted into the weapon. Charging or preparing the weapon for firing requires racking and releasing the slide.

Semi-automatic pistols come available in single-action and double-action, similar to revolvers. For some semi-automatic pistols, when the slide is retracted it also cocks the hammer. This makes the gun ready to fire with a single-action type of pull. On other pistols, the trigger must be pulled to cock the hammer and then the weapon will fire similar to a double-action revolver. Some may have a safety lever that can be used to block the gun from firing. Others may have a de-cocking lever to safely lower the hammer.

Features vary from model to model. A knowledgeable salesperson can review the details while you are shopping.

Caliber Choices

It's easier to select a caliber than handgun model. Even so, the choice of one influences the other. For first-time gun owners, most experts suggest choosing one of the more common calibers. They are normally less expensive and fit within a budget allowing you to purchase bulk ammo for practice.

For revolvers, consider the .38 Special, .38 Special +P and .357 Magnum. The top choices for semi-autos are the .380 ACP, 9mm, .40 S&W and .45 ACP. While there are many more caliber choices available, the standard choices are best suited for beginners.

One case in point is the .380 ACP. This cartridge is basically a small version of the 9mm. Both use the same diameter bullet, but the case is shorter on the .380. It's also underpowered when compared to the 9mm. Some may tell you that it kicks less and is easier to shoot, although that is not necessarily the case.

'Kick' is a common term used when discussing recoil. A bullet generates force in both directions when the projectile leaves the barrel. Recoil or kick is the force coming back in the direction of the shooter. This is where handgun choice ties into caliber selection.

The heavier the weapon, the less recoil the shooter will feel. For the sake of this discussion, we can compare that

to the 9mm. This round will generate a certain amount of power when fired. If the handgun weighs two pounds, then it takes more power to push it back than if it only weighs one pound. Thus, the shooter feels less of a push. Most .380 ACP handguns are rather small and many times the felt recoil will be greater than a 9mm round shot in a slightly larger handgun.

Why give up the power for a few ounces of weight? Remember, given the same cartridge, the small gun will have a greater kick. Most new shooters can learn to handle any of the listed calibers if they use the right handgun and have proper guidance.

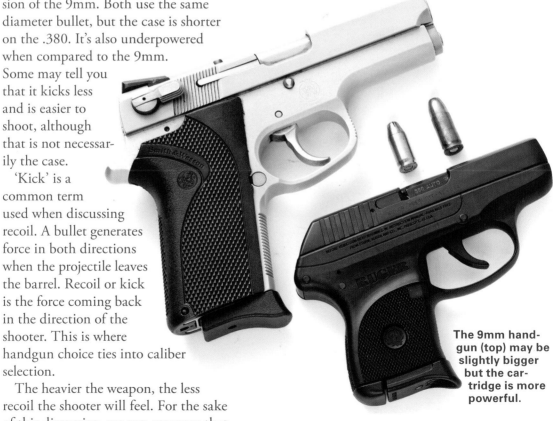

The 9mm handgun (top) may be slightly bigger but the cartridge is more powerful.

Download the owner's manual from the website of a reputable handgun maker. You can read about the gun under consideration before making a costly purchase.

Online Research

After you've made your list, it's time to do more research. Internet research can also pay off in helping you to make the best decision based on your needs for concealed-carry.

The websites maintained by Smith & Wesson and Sturm, Ruger & Co. and other gun makers allow you to download the owner's manual for their brands and guns. The manuals are logical teaching tools and can instruct you in the operation of the firearms. Manuals offer a good section on gun safety and should be read prior to handling a firearm. They will give you a head start prior to your trip to a gun shop.

Shopping Tips

We're almost to the fun part. You have one more task to complete before going shopping for a new firearm. Review the phone book or Internet and make a list of gun shops in your area. Some gun shops have an indoor range where you can rent firearms to test various weapons, see how they fit your hand and thus find the best one for you. Although you may have to pay for the bullets used and the time spent at the range, most will find the benefits worth the cost.

You might want to call before your initial visit to find out the least busy time the shop and range are open. Explain that you are new to firearms and ask for help. Gun shops are normally friendly places and the salespeople don't mind spending time chatting with customers.

Ask to handle different sizes of revolvers and semi-automatics to see which feels the best in your hand. Fit is just as important in handguns as with a new pair of shoes. Ask the salesperson to explain each function and ask him or her if you can try to operate an empty firearm. Take notes and bring your list.

Buying a gun on your first trip is not the goal. While you are at the shop, ask if they offer safety or beginner classes. If not, they might know of a resource in the area.

Your first day of shopping for a handgun is where your sixth sense comes into play. Normally you will be able to tell how sincere a person is about helping you. You will also get a feel of the level of knowledge of the salesperson. He or she should be willing to show you several models and explain each model in detail. A good salesperson will know the importance of finding just the right firearm. A salesperson can tell you what legalities are required to purchase a handgun. Each state has its own process and the gun shop can provide all the details. Don't hesitate to visit every shop in the area. The next shop down the road may have the perfect firearm for you. You wouldn't buy an automobile without test-driving at more than one dealer. Your handgun shopping should have the same importance.

This is also the time to talk with friends and relatives. They may have firearms that you can try and may be able to offer additional advice. Keep in mind that just because they have a handgun does not mean they are knowledgeable. Only you can decide which gun makes the best fit for you.

While searching, if you found classes to attend, now is the time to go. You may have to put the classes off until after you purchase a firearm. However, many instructors have handguns you can use until you purchase your own. At the same time, don't forget that gun shopping can be a two-person endeavor. You may have a friend that has the same interest and you can offer each other support throughout the learning process.

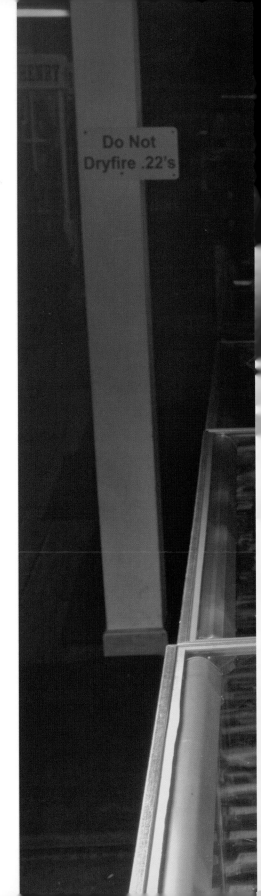

Some gun shops have indoor ranges available to customers. Take advantage of that option prior to purchasing the gun.

Price Tag

Cost is the final factor in selecting the perfect handgun. Cost is a relative factor when shopping for a handgun. The old adage of "you get what you pay for" definitely comes into play, but don't feel as if you have to buy the most expensive handgun on the market. Even the major handgun companies have a great variance in price from model to model.

First, shop the major brand names in the handgun market and then select the model that best fits your needs. Cost does not play a factor when you are trying to choose between which action type is best for you. If you select a particular model and you find that one shop doesn't carry it, ask if they can order it for you and inquire about the cost. An important point to remember is that most shops are privately owned so pricing will vary. When discussing price, don't hesitate to ask if the price tag is the bottom line.

Gun store employees are gun owners. They can be a helpful resource when deciding on which gun works best for you. Here, Franklin Gun Shop owner, Brian Hassler assists a new customer.

9: Accessorize

Ammunition, magazines and carrying cases are just a few of the necessary items needed to go with a handgun.

The Complete Package

A husband comes home after a day of shopping. The wife asks what he bought. He responds: "A handgun, gun case, cleaning kit, holster and gun belt."

The wife's response: "You bought all of that?"

The wife comes home after a day of shopping. Her take for the day is a handbag, skirt, blouse, pair of shoes and belt. The husband asks what she bought. She answers: "Not much, just one outfit."

To a woman, an outfit is often a singular item. She knows that accessorizing comes as part of the purchase. Make no doubt about it, when it comes to accessorizing, a stylish woman puts a man to shame. For those reasons, it's surprising to many gun retailers that women don't rule the firearm market.

You've made the decision to purchase a firearm, but will soon discover the handgun is just part of the total package. Owning a handgun means you need to own a series of other products to help guarantee your weapon stays in good working order. Call this process "accessorizing the handgun."

101

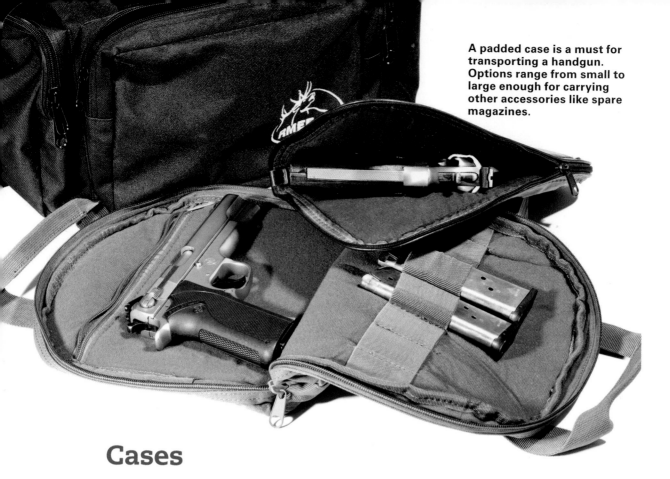

A padded case is a must for transporting a handgun. Options range from small to large enough for carrying other accessories like spare magazines.

Cases

While shopping for ammunition, you can peruse the choices of small padded gun cases. You must store your gun somewhere, as the last thing you want is to leave it out in the open. Choosing the place to store the weapon takes thought. If you use a firearm for home defense, you'll want to store it where you can get to it, but also away from untrained hands, especially children.

It is important to purchase a padded case for storage and transportation. Manufacturers produce several variations of cases and some even have space for extra ammunition or magazines. Remember a closed case may attract condensation when exposed to temperature changes. This problem can become severe when a gun is stored in a vehicle, as temperature can vary and fluctuate. In the summer, the problem worsens if direct sunlight shines

on the gun. If you plan on storing your gun in a case, keep it unzipped or slightly open to prevent this problem, as it's easy to close the case when carrying it.

Another option to consider is a small range bag. These bags are similar in size to a camera case. Many carry permit holders use them to carry handguns, ammunition and other accessories to and from the range for practice sessions. A good range bag has a compartment dedicated for a handgun and keeps the gun from banging against other items. Depending on the choice, a good range bag can pull double duty as a storage case.

Some shooters prefer discreet carrying cases that hide the fact that they're carrying a gun. Others prefer a hard case that gives an added layer of protection. It's important to get a case that secures your gun and protects it from damage.

Ammunition

Surprisingly, you shouldn't place a gun holster at the top of your shopping list and instead focus your attention on ammunition. The number of companies making ammunition is practically as large as the number of companies making handguns. At the same time, ammunition companies offer several different selections in the same caliber based on bullet weight, powder load and bullet type. For instance, Hornady Manufacturing Co. and Federal Premium Ammunition offer a collective 26 different loads and counting for the .38 Special/.357 Magnum combination.

Major companies have ammunition labeled for a particular use, meaning you can match selection to your need. For most economical shooters, that comes down to having one load for defensive use and a milder target load for practice. The mild target loads typically cost less and are shot the most. You might even purchase ammunition from lesser-known companies for practice loads if it saves you significant cost. However, always stay with one of the major companies for your defensive loads.

Be sure the ammunition you buy matches the caliber of the gun.

103

Eye and Ears

Anytime you fire a weapon you should use both eye and ear protection. While earmuff-style ear protection might not do much for your hairstyle, most experienced shooters can attest hearing damage is not worth shooting without them. Fire just a couple of shots without protection and you'll likely hear a ringing in your ears for hours, which signifies hearing damage. Hearing damage can also accumulate over time and become permanent in old age.

The law requires all earmuff manufacturers to list their decibel reduction rating on the package. Most earmuffs cost little compared to the consequence of hearing loss and damage.

Earplugs are another option. They come in various forms, ranging from simple, soft sponge earbuds to types custom formed. When it comes to your hearing safety, go with the best you can afford.

Eye protection is just as important. Shooters should always wear impact resistant safety glasses when firing a weapon. Glass can protect you from splatter, which occurs when a bullet strikes a hard target and breaks up and fragments fly in all directions.

Safety glasses come in various styles, including sunglasses many shooters find stylish enough to wear away from shooting environments.

Eyewear for shooting is both functional and stylish. Some shooting glasses can be worn as sunglasses.

A quality and properly fitted holster gives shooters the ability to easily and quickly access their gun in a life-threatening situation.

Eye Muffs™

Holsters

The time for using a holster for concealed carry use is when you carry the gun on your person. Firearm owners should not store their gun in a holster for a number of reasons.

Most manufacturers use leather to make holsters. Though aesthetically pleasing, over time leather will cause a firearm to corrode, as the material absorbs moisture. When combined with chemicals used in the tanning process, leather holsters can ultimately result in damaging a handgun's finish. Leather is still one of the better materials for a holster, but you should take care to keep the holster dry. Most quality leather holsters have suede lining that produces less wear on a weapon's finish. Companies also produce nylon and plastic holsters, which would work as good substitute to leather holsters. When shopping, remember holsters don't come in one-size-fits-all and a good holster should perfectly and snugly fit your handgun.

Like shoes, holsters serve various functions. A holster designed for combat or hunting shouldn't double as a holster used for concealed carry, as their designs vary too drastically. Instead, choose a holster suited for the gun's intended use. Many gun owners have have two or three holsters for a single handgun and switch them out when using their handgun in different settings.

Level of retention is another important feature of a holster. The handgun needs to stay in the holster until its intended time of use. Thus, a handgun shouldn't fall out of its holster if you run or physically exert yourself. Take time to break in a new holster the same way you would a new pair of shoes. You want the gun to fit securely, but drawing the gun should remain relatively easy in case of emergency.

Fortunately, the firearm industry has realized people come in all sizes. As many seek to protect themselves against unexpected threats, more and more women have begun carrying firearms to protect themselves and their loved ones. Because of this, holsters now come in a host of different varieties, makes and models to accommodate all body types and figures. If in an urban environment, it is unwise to wear a clearly visible handgun. However, it is logical to keep your gun in a specially designed purse or bag. Handbag makers have designed options for transporting a firearm. If using a handbag, ensure it has a separate compartment for the handgun so you can easily access it during a threatening situation.

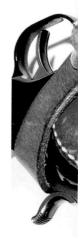

Holsters vary by size but also application. You want a holster that keeps the gun secure for concealed carry use.

Holster belts are designed to balance the additional weight of a weapon.

Belts

Many concealed carry newcomers overlook using belts to obscure their weapon. The typical belts simply hold up your pants and nothing more. You need more strength with the added weight of a firearm. The usual gun belt with the cartridge loops may be fine for you in the field, but you may want something less obvious for concealed carry.

Many holster companies offer a wide selection of quality-made belts. They are normally better quality than belts offered at a department store, but don't worry about looking like a cowboy at high noon, as most holsters and belts now come in stylish, modern designs.

Cleaning Kits

When accessorizing your handgun, one should also purchase a good gun cleaning kit. Every time one fires their gun, carbon deposits build up on the surface of a handgun and down the barrel. Bullets may also leave lead or copper deposits in the barrel, depending on the type of bullet fired. Over time, these deposits can affect the function of the weapon. A quality lubricant and cleaner will clean the gun of these deposits, prevent rust and lubricate the gun's moving parts. Thus, consider a cleaning kit a necessity and use it after every trip to the range.

Review the owner's manual for pertinent information about cleaning your gun. Most manuals cover the proper disassembly and cleaning of a handgun.

Make sure the accessories of a cleaning kit fit the caliber of your handgun.

Gun Ranges and Training Courses

First-time gun owners may find the first day at the range a bit nerve racking and a somewhat anxious experience. Women may feel more intimidated. While one can expect a certain level of nervousness, one should temper these feelings and not let these emotions get in the way of visiting the range or shooting your handgun. Like the first day of school, these nervous feelings quickly fade and one will soon feel at home at the range. This first experience at the range only comes once, so try relaxing, making the most of it and enjoying yourself. While you are a beginner once, you are a student for life.

Student of the Gun

Paul G. Markel, one of the writer's of this book, is a full-time small arms and tactics instructor. In 1987 he joined the U.S. Marines and then spent 17 years as a police officer. Today, Markel writes and host *Student of the Gun*, an educational and entertainment-focused TV series on The Sportsman Channel. On the show, Markel further details much of his advice concerning gun safety and shooting. The following pages serve as an introduction and survey of some of Markel's most essential and needed advice.

Read the Directions

In order to have the most productive and enjoyable first day at the range, one should properly prepare themselves before stepping onto a live-fire situation. First, take the gun out of the box and set it aside. Remove the owner's manual and open it. Read it thoroughly from beginning to end. The reason for this is simple: Who knows a product better than the people who made it? The firearm's manufacturer might have some important tips regarding the operation and characteristics of your gun. Additionally, you might even discover features and information about your gun you didn't know it had.

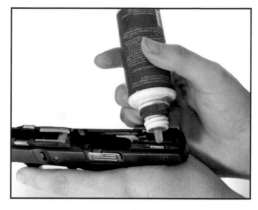

Any place on the firearm where metal is moving against other metal needs lubrication.

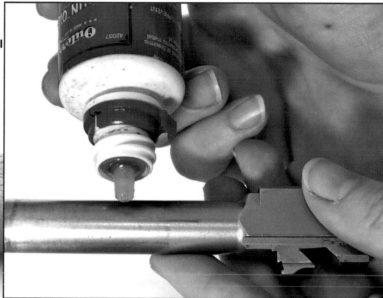

Reading the owner's manual teaches you two important lessons: how to use the gun and an explanation of gun features.

Gun Check

Check the gun inside and out. If the rails and moving parts appear dry, then apply a small amount of lubricant or oil, but you don't want liquid dripping from the gun. Be aware of the chamber and slide face, as only the lightest amount of oil is necessary to keep these parts in good working condition. As mentioned, quality lubricants and cleaning products can remove carbon and dirt build-up.

Keep in mind that a gun is a simple machine and machines work best when clean and well lubricated. Also take time to familiarize yourself with your gun's operating features. With the ammunition in a separate room, spend time working the action and locating and using the manual controls. Point the gun in a safe direction, press the trigger, and hold the gun as still as possible.

Ensure the ammunition you purchase for your firearm is appropriate for that particular gun.

Ammunition Check

Check the manufacturer's ammunition recommendation. Ensure the ammunition you purchase for your firearm is appropriate for your gun. There are "+P" and "+P+" types of ammunition that have a heavier powder charge. Not all firearms can accept or use these loads, despite the fact they may indeed chamber these rounds. It's important to take along more ammunition than you anticipate using at the range, as you can always bring home what goes unused.

Think of it another way: you don't want to end your day early if you don't bring enough ammunition and anticipate using a lot of ammunition when practicing and training. This is particularly true if attending your very first training course. Because you took the time and effort to sign up for the course, ensure you bring enough ammunition to shoot and thus get the most out of your time with an instructor.

Training is what you do under the watchful eye of a professional instructor. Practice is what you do at your home range after you have some competent instruction.

My First Gun School

Now is the time to think about taking a professional training course or even enrolling in a shooting school. There are innumerable private firearms academies throughout the nation. Many will find attending a professional firearms training program one of the greatest experiences they can have in furthering their skills with a handgun.

Though beneficial, some may find making the decision to sign up for the class the most difficult part of the process, as the classes do command some time. Gun train-ing instructors hear the same excuses from prospective students on why they've procrastinated signing up for a formal course. Some say they want to take a course, but hold off because they want to practice shooting before enrolling. A lack of experience shouldn't deter a person from taking a shooting class, as you attend to learn how and what to practice when shooting. We would also stress you cannot practice your way of training, as training and true instruction should only occur under the watchful eye of a professional or experienced instructor. Practice is what you do at your home range after you have competent instruction. Thus, one shouldn't feel obligated to shoot 500 rounds in preparation for a training course. By doing this, a new shooter can also ingrain themselves with bad habits they will end up correcting during their training course. Instead of worrying about your skill level, take time to prepare your mind, body and gear. Dedicated preparation time goes a long way toward ensuring you have a productive training session.

115

Preparing for Gun Camp

Each year, thousands of citizens exercise their right to bear arms as guaranteed by the Second Amendment. Many begin by taking part in training courses offered at any number of professional firearms schools and academies. Most will find participating in formal training a definite and worthwhile investment. Shooters devote time and money to seek out experts with the knowledge, experience and expertise to provide instruction they can't get at home. Planning a trip to a shooting school is a big deal, as it often requires one to block out the time, cash and even some vacation days to attend. From a monetary standpoint, you must factor the price of tuition, travel, lodging, meals and ammunition. With all these things in mind, get the most for your time by ensuring you have the proper gear, clothing, accessories and weapon before arriving at your training course.

Each year thousands of citizens exercise their constitutionally guaranteed right to bear arms. They begin by taking part in training courses.

Train in real-world environments. If a life-threatening situation arises, you will likely not be able to get a perfect stance in a perfectly lit room with a perfect angle. Train to shoot behind cover and in low light areas.

Head to Toe

While at a training course, cold, wet and sore feet can distract you from learning. Focus starts from the ground up, so ensure you have comfortable, well-fitting boots or shoes.

Take it a step further to get the most from your experience and avoid mental distractions. Pack two pairs of footwear you can use at the gun range, as most training schools operate rain or shine and you can expect to be outside training unless lightning develops. If your boots get soaked the first day, they likely won't dry by the next morning when you need them. Thus, bring a backup pair of closed-toed shoes or boots so you can avoid wearing wet boots.

Regarding weather, take the time to research the average temperature and weather forecast for the area where the training session will occur. Think layers. Cold mornings in the high desert quickly give way to hot afternoons. Conversely, a sunny morning in the Midwest can easily become a rainy afternoon. You'll never regret taking a quality rain jacket with an insulated liner, though many find it easy to forget packing such an essential item. Regardless of the weather, shooters should always favor long sleeve shirts and pants more than shorts and short sleeve shirts. Hot brass will fly from guns, which can burn bare skin, but one can avoid this when properly covered. New shooters should also consider investing in knee pads, as some classes require dynamic marksmanship training that goes beyond standing and shooting a target.

Being sure to pack clothes for comfort and practicality is the key to being prepared for a gun school.

Her Story: First Day at the Range

As mentioned, Paul G. Markel has taught thousands of people — many of them women — through his various training courses and television show. He's no stranger to watching anxious women step up to the firing point for the very first time. Below Markel's fellow outdoor journalist Britney Starr accounts her first day at the range. Starr is managing editor of Women's Outdoor News.

"My dad is a retired Michigan State Police officer. He introduced me to firearms as soon as I was able to safely handle them. I was pretty fearless when it came to following in his footsteps and shooting .45-caliber handguns by the time I hit my teenage years. The first time I shot a handgun, I felt a lot of fulfillment knowing I was making my dad proud. Shooting together also created a very close bond between us. Now when I shoot, I still feel empowered, but also feel confident I can safely defend myself if necessary."

Packing the proper safety gear such as ear muffs is an essential part of packing for a gun school.

Read the List

Many men learn through visuals and hands-on experience. Though easy to overlook, men and women alike should read the recommended gear list provided by their shooting school. Instructors at these schools teach handgun safety and shootings for a living and thus new shooters should heed their advice, particularly concerning gear. Most professional shooting academies don't allow shoulder holsters and crossdraw rigs on their ranges, which your instructor will likely note in their preliminary instructions to the course. If the school recommends you bring at least three magazines for your pistol, don't try to shortcut them and bring one or two. Simply, a shooter should bring more than enough magazines and not get caught ill-prepared. Regarding gear, especially magazines, take time to mark them with a Sharpie pen before going to the school. Write your name on each magazine, as it would increase the likelihood of getting them back should they get lost or misplaced. Also ensure you have the correct safety gear by packing wrap-around shooting glasses and protective earmuffs. Many will also find investing in a good pair electronic hearing protection worthwhile, as they further protect hearing. These electronic hearing earmuffs also relieve some of the frustration of not hearing your teacher's instructions while shooting, as they obscure loud noises but also allow shooters to hear the human voice.

Physical Fitness

Most shooting schools don't require substantial or prolonged physical activity. Nonetheless, one should expect to exert some physical effort. At the very least, you'll spend a lot of time on your feet. If you have a genuine physical disability or handicap, discuss this with your instructors beforehand so they can accommodate your needs. Additionally, one should begin exercising regularly or stay in decent shape before taking a shooting class. Remember, a shooting class is an investment and one should try and make the most of the experience.

120

Expert Advice

Planning a trip to a professional firearms academy is a bit of an adventure and usually requires one to leave their comfort zone, which is a good. It's nearly impossible for shooters to grow or improve in any area or endeavor without professional guidance or honest peer critique.

Paul Howe, a retired U.S. Army Master Sergeant and current owner of Combat Shooting and Tactics school, has written: "Training, like selection, is a never ending process. We begin learning on day one of our life."

While new shooters can expect the freshman jitters, these feelings only happen once and quickly disappear. If you slow down, take some time to familiarize yourself with your new gun and gear, you can help rid yourself of some initial nervousness.

Like most new shooters, you'll likely not forget nor regret your first professional firearms course.

Attitude Check

Attitude is the most critical factor in determining how much benefit you get from a formal training course. The type and value of the gun in hand is worthless unless your mind is sharp, focused and trained on what you are doing at the moment.

Paul G. Markel, the writer of this chapter, interviewed some of the nation's top firearms instructors. His question was the same with each expert inquiry. Markel wanted to know the one bit of advice they could give freshmen students of gun training courses. Here's what those experts had to share with Markel, a fellow instructor. Each answer came down to the same common topic. Attitude.

Dave Starin, Gunsite Academy training administrator: "Improper gear or clothing can lead to mental distraction and even breakdown. On the other side of that coin is the misconception that different gear or clothing will solve unrelated problems such as improper trigger control or sight alignment. These two areas are usually the easiest to remedy. Mental preparedness or mindset can enable students to overcome the gear, improper clothes and physical limitations."

John Benner, owner of Tactical Defense Institute: "Mental preparedness is the most important. We rarely have an issue but people need to go to a class with an open mind and try their best to do as the instructor asks, obviously as long as it is safe. It is an individual's choice about what methods and techniques they adopt. But when you go to someone's class, you have chosen to do that for a reason. Try what they are teaching. I never want anyone to feel they can't ask a question, although we always try to explain that ahead of time."

Shane Iversen, the Senior Instructor for the Texas Pistol Academy: "Attitude is the basis for self defense. Not an attitude of arrogance or swagger, but an attitude of confidence based on martial competency."

11: Gun Range Etiquette

Many shooters fail to realize the importance of range etiquette. Incidents resulting in injury on a firearms range often stem from a shooter's failure to know, understand or practice proper range etiquette. It's all about safety and following the rules. While one should certainly enjoy shooting their firearm, all shooters must remember firearms possess life ending power and demand respect. Even small pistols can cause significant injury or even death when improperly used. Mistakes with firearms are seldom forgiving, but following the rules provided makes shooting firearms as safe as possible. These rules have become well established among experienced firearm users and any new shooter would benefit from committing them to remember and implementing them at the shooting range.

Multiple shooters at the firing line of a gun range make following the rules important.

Safety Basics

Practical application and experience has birthed most range rules and guidelines. Like most rules in life, one can often attribute incidents to failure to follow said rules. While range rules may not always make sense to new shooters, it is critical to follow them to ensure everyones' safety. Doing so protects you, other shooters and bystanders.

Range and shooting environments differ as do civilian range rules and rules at competitive events. Military and law enforcement ranges can also vary depending on the weapons used and the training environment. Most shooters find these differences relatively minor with two primary range classifications: hot (loaded) and cold (unloaded).

Always follow the range master's instructions when on the firing line at a gun range.

The Rules

Most casual shooters using a public facility will encounter a cold range. As one might assume, cold refers to the condition of the handgun, not the weather. A "cold" handgun is one that remains completely unloaded. When not in use, cold guns have all their ammunition removed, including the magazine. Most competition ranges use this condition to maintain participants utmost safety.

Those who operate public range facilities generally keep them strongly controlled with clear, restrictive rules. Inexperienced shooters often populate these ranges and one or two rangemasters typically observe public ranges. Without strict rules, rangemasters couldn't maintain everyone's safety.

Public ranges control when and where you can handle, load and fire your weapon. Handling can only occur on the shooting bench with no holstered weapons allowed. Most public ranges forbid shooters to practice drawing their gun, stand or sit at the bench and only permit firing from a standing, normal position. Shooters can only move cased weapons on and off the shooting line, set targets at specific time and no one is allowed in front of the shooting line when others shoot. When setting targets, no one is allowed near his or her firearm. A range master will control all shooting conditions and will direct when each step of the shooting, reloading and target setting occurs.

Shooters using a public facility will most likely come across a cold range. This means that when not in use, handguns should have all ammunition removed, including the magazine.

Competitive Rules

Most competitive events are also cold, but have a few different rules. Shooters need to draw from the holster, move during firing and switch from range to range. Ranges design different rules to accommodate this movement while ensuring safety for those not shooting.

A competitive range only allows cased or holstered weapons. Shooters may not remove the weapon from the holster or case unless on the firing line or at a designated work area. At all other times, shooters must keep their gun cased or in a holster. One only loads their weapon at the shooting line when preparing for each stage of the event. Those participating will load prior to starting the stage and unload prior to leaving. The range doesn't allow anyone to leave the firing line with a loaded weapon and the range master will often have shooters remove their magazine, hold the slide open (or open the cylinder on a revolver), inspect it, close the slide and press the trigger, guaranteeing the chamber has no live rounds.

Competitive events can have hundreds of shooters with various experience levels moving about the range. Strict rules are the only way event organizers can reasonably ensure a safe environment for all.

Some training academies and organizations follow a modified cold range. Most will either encourage or forbid handling weapons at the car. Training involves several "strings" or "courses" of fire, all of which occur on a firing line or designated range. In some cases, you'll never leave the firing line with a loaded weapon. Others will keep you "hot" until you leave the range. A course's instructor will determine the restrictiveness of their training range. For the most part, keep your weapon unloaded when not shooting.

The range master controls where you load and unload your weapon. That makes paying attention important at all times.

127

Staying Hot

As you might expect, a "hot" range means weapons remain loaded while on the range. Many encounter this type of range at police ranges, training academies or occasionally at military practice ranges. However, these ranges still enforce rules. In fact, shooters should consider a hot range's rules even more critical than those of a cold range, as they approximate real world conditions.

Shooters should note the designated areas for handling weapons at a hot range. Most rangemasters and course operators discourage or prohibit handling weapons in the parking lot or at one's car. Once the gun is in your holster, you may only draw it on the firing line or at a designated area. Once holstered, leave your gun alone until you're on the line or at the designated handling area.

Most facilities will allow you to unload your weapon prior to leaving the range for a personal break. Most often, rangemasters require shooters to unloaded their weapons at the firing line. In many cases, this training is for experienced concealed carry holders.

Following these instructions provides you the best training and familiarization when carrying a weapon in public.

Safety Check

Ranges and training facilities may have conditions varying from what this book describes. Some private facilities may even have no rules at all. If you come across a private facility without rules, follow one of the protocols already mentioned. If rules don't dictate the condition of the range (hot or cold), shooters should still use extreme discretion when firing and handling their firearm and use proper range etiquette. Following these simple rules can ensure your safety even if no one is watching. Shooters should also encourage a safe and friendly range environment, as, while fun, shooting guns has its dangers.

To ensure everyone's safety, shooters should follow the rules while shooting at a range. A range master will direct a shooter when to shoot, reload and set targets.

Practice versus Training

As mentioned, training only occurs under the watchful eye of a professional instructor. New shooters cannot successfully train themselves and hope to become skilled, responsible shooters and gun carriers. Many professional firearm trainers operate under the belief that proper training teaches new shooters what to practice on their own time to become more skilled with their weapon.

Thus, practice occurs when away from an instructor. Think of practice as a skill maintenance endeavor, as even professional shooters still regularly practice. In fact, one can often determine the difference between an amateur and a professional shooter by the amount of time they spend practicing.

Step one in this chapter is committing to professional training. A second or third pair of eyes watching you can help reduce your learning curve and make you a better, more competent shooter.

Practice and train. Too often, shooters use those words interchangeably. The beginning of this chapter will review shooting framework and establish some basic training ground rules, but one should remember practice and training are separate and equally important. Experienced shooters can attest that shooting a gun requires both physical and mental commitment. Over time, one's shooting skill will deteriorate, just as with any other physical skill. Thus, mastery of any physical endeavor — shooting a weapon chief among these — requires education, training and dedicated practice.

Practicing is what you do on your own, with hours spent at the range following up on the training skills learned from an instructor.

Marksmanship Fundamentals

What and how you practice depends on one's level of training and experience. A freshman outfielder practices differently than a professional. However, both athletes work on the fundamentals.

Take time to focus on shooting fundamentals before venturing out on the range for the very first time. Take your time and deliberately go slow. Speed doesn't count when learning the fundamentals of shooting. The world's very best shooters still practice the fundamentals.

New shooters trying to master fundamentals should first recognize the importance of consistency. All shooters will find mental discipline the key to good marksmanship and repeatable shot success. Mastering the fundamentals begins with a repetitive process. Step-by-step instructions follow.

How you practice begins with training and experience, achieved through instruction.

The front sight should remain the eyes' primary focus when engaging a target.

Front Sight

Of a handgun's two sights, the front sight is the most important, as the human eye can only focus on one object at a time. Because of this, shooters should focus on the front sight and let the rear sight remain blurry or out of focus when firing their weapon. The front sight should stay perfectly clear until the shot breaks.

Trigger Press

A smooth, deliberate trigger press ensures the rounds group together in a consistent manner. Only the pad or fingerprint area of the trigger finger should make direct contact with the trigger surface. Don't quickly jerk the trigger, but instead slowly and smoothly squeeze the trigger until the gun fires.

The pad or fingerprint area of the trigger finger is the portion that should make direct contact with the trigger surface.

Practicing the fundamentals of shooting begins with consistency. Mastering fundamentals is a repetitive process that demands substantial practice.

Follow Through

Many shooters refer to this process as riding the recoil. Sight alignment and sight picture occur after the shot breaks and the shooter's eye reacquires the front sight. Shooters should keep proper sight picture on the front sight after firing, as it will help them quickly find the target for additional shots.

Every repeating firearm has a mechanical trigger reset. That is a point where the trigger/sear is reset so the gun can be fired again.

Trigger Reset

Beginners often naturally remove their finger from the trigger when their gun discharges. By doing this, these shooters must again place their finger on the trigger, adjust to the correct firing position and perform another complete trigger stroke. The additional movement of again finding the trigger adds unneeded motion to the shooting process and reduces the likelihood of a well placed follow-up shot.

Every repeating firearm has a mechanical trigger reset, which is a point where the sear resets so the shooter can again fire the gun. After firing, a shooter should only let off the trigger enough to reset the sear. By mastering the trigger reset, shooters can eliminate unnecessary motion or physical pressure on the gun that disturbs the sights. As every firearm is different, we'd encourage new and experienced shooters alike to work with their gun to find its trigger reset.

A two-handed grip is the most secure and offers the greatest stability.

Mastering the fundamentals takes time on the gun range.

Grip

Shooters need a solid grip to control their gun and accurately shoot. Most firearm experts would agree that gripping a firearm with two hands offers the greatest stability. Begin with the dominant hand and grasp the handgun high on the frame or on the backstrap area. After the dominant hand is in place, cup the support around the dominant hand and try to best align the knuckles. The ultimate effect should have the shooter placing as much of their hands on the gun as possible.

The support hand wraps the shooting hand with the fingers wrapping around each other.

The grip should feel like a firm handshake, but shooters shouldn't hold the gun so tightly that blood leaves the fingers or the hands tremble. For pistols and revolvers, the shooter should stack his or her thumbs one on the other with the shooting hand's thumb on top. Point both thumbs in the direction of the target.

Practice Fundamentals

Mastering the fundamentals takes time and repetition. Once you have a clear understanding of both, you can further your gun skills even more by attending a shooters' school. Paul Markel — one of the authors of this book — runs a popular shooting school that is part of his *Student of the Gun* show and educational series. One of the exercises Markel introduces to his students he calls the One Box Work-out™. The 50-round practice routine helps shooters make the most of their time and available ammunition.

The One Box Workout is simple, as one only requires 50 rounds of ammunition, a target and no special equipment. While ammunition has never been cheap, today it costs more than at any other time in recent memory. For dedicated and new shooters alike, most will find making the most of every round fired the key to successful shooting.

One Box Workout

Step 1

Begin with a single box of 50 rounds of training ammunition. To begin the drill you load 10 rounds in the gun or load it to capacity if the gun doesn't hold 10 rounds.

With your target set at 5 to 7 yards, begin with a two-hand grip and slow-fire the first magazine or cylinder. Take your time and focus on a smooth, deliberate trigger press and clear front sight. This is not a speed drill. It is a fundamentals drill. However long it takes to place 10 well-aimed shots on the target is the amount of time you will need.

Step 2

Reload your handgun and repeat the first drill, but this time fire all rounds only using your dominant hand. Hold your non-dominant hand close to your chest and take your time to focus on solid marksmanship fundamentals. One of the keys to success when shooting single-handed is ensuring your wrist is locked. As you fire, also focus on the front sight.

Step 3

Continue the practice session. Reload the handgun and fire the next exercise using your support or off hand only. Focus intently on the front sight and smoothly press the trigger.

Remember to lock the wrist so the gun doesn't move around. Conduct this step of the workout with diligence and deliberation, as it demonstrates your ability with the non-dominant hand.

Step 4

If your practice range forbids the use of a holster, simply set the gun on the shelf or table, as you shouldn't time your draw speed during this drill. Shooters should practice slow, deliberate action when performing this drill.

With the handgun loaded and holstered, smoothly draw and engage the target. Fire two shots and then slowly re-holster the gun. Repeat the drill until emptying the gun. Stage the gun on the table and take a step back. On command, step forward, pick up the gun and fire two or three shots at the target. Reset and try again.

Step 5

Empty your magazines down to two, three or four rounds. Begin with a partially loaded handgun and engage the target until the gun runs dry and reload it. Focus on making very deliberate and methodical actions. Repeat the drill two or three more times. Most will find this drill difficult with a revolver, but possible with a speed-loader or quick strip.

This last exercise should likely finish your 50 rounds. If you have ammunition remaining, repeat whichever drill you found the most difficult. You don't improve by doing what you've mastered, but only become better by practicing areas you find challenging.

Try the One Box Workout the next time at the practice range. It's a great way to make the most of your available time and ammunition.

Indoor Range Tips

Depending on location, some shooters may only have access to an indoor range for training and practice. In this case, take time to examine the indoor shooting range. You might discover how to get the most out of time at the firing line.

Lights

Shooters can benefit from an indoor range that allows practicing with tactical lights and laser sights, though few outdoor ranges allow shooting after sundown. Given the opportunity, working with the light/gun combination at an indoor range will give you an opportunity to practice properly using the gear. An indoor range setting allows you to see the white beam from a gun-mounted light.

Shooters have a number of different ways to use a handheld light in conjunction with a firearm, among these the Modified FBI, the Neck-Index and Harries techniques.

Using a handheld light with a live firearm is not a skill you simply pick up, as it requires a fair amount of practice and even professional training. When practicing flashlight techniques, you should first work on form. Speed will come after a shooter has a good handle on carrying and using a light.

If you have a pistol with an accessory rail and a light mounted directly to the frame, you'll likely find handing your gun much easier, as both hands can stay on the grip. The activator switch location and operation for your weapon light will vary depending on the model and manufacturer.

An indoor range offers the best environment to clearly see laser sights in operation.

Lasers

An indoor range offers the best environment to clearly see laser sights in operation. The sun can wash out red lasers, but newer green lasers stay more visible during the day.

Most will find visible laser sights helpful when shooting indoors, under poor lighting conditions or when firing from an awkward position. Laser sights prove challenging for many gun owners because they sometimes feel laser sights negate the need for practice, though untrue. Poor trigger control is poor trigger control with or without a laser.

Just as with any type of equipment, those with laser sights should frequent the shooting range for practice. Again, most will find an indoor range the perfect setting for working with laser sights.

Working the Gun

An indoor or outdoor range setting provides a good opportunity to work on gun handling skills, which often involves manipulating a firearm's manual controls.

Depending on the make and model, your handgun could have any number of manual controls. These manual controls may include de-cocking levers, manual safeties, slide locks, cylinder releases and other features, though every manufacturer puts their special touch on these areas. For instance, the Beretta 92 and SIG P226 both have de-cocking levers, but place them differently on the gun.

While at the range, take time to thoroughly familiarize yourself with your guns controls so you can effectively use the weapon in a self-defense situation.

Take time at the range to learn about the manual controls on your gun.

Target Considerations

While it might seem simplistic, the target you shoot can influence your practice sessions' level of success. First, most will find it worthwhile to understand the composition and various types of targets.

Manufacturers typically make targets out of paper, cardboard, plastic and steel. The generic paper target is the most common and inexpensive, though susceptible to wind. When used outdoors, secure these targets to a proper backing or staple them to plywood or similar material.

Most shooters will find a target with a circle or bullseye target appropriate for working on basic marksmanship fundamentals. However, if practicing with self-defense in mind, you may want to practice with a silhouette target. Shooters have various options from which to choose, such as a black and white silhouette or a full-color human silhouette.

Some companies even produce three-dimensional plastic targets providing an even better representation of a human attacker. Likewise, shooters can drape an old t-shirt over their targets for a more realistic approach.

Steel targets offer several advantages for practice. Steel lasts nearly forever and shooters can fire into this material repeatedly before it needs replacing. Steel targets also offer instant feedback. When you hear the audible 'clang' of a bullet striking steel, no question remains as to whether or not you hit or missed the target. Also, you don't need to walk down range to check your shot holes as you would with a paper target.

Angle the steel targets down toward the ground at approximately 20 degrees. This helps direct bullet splatter safely toward the deck. Every reputable manufacturer of reactive steel targets has "Recommend Safe Distance" guidelines. Shooters should read and follow guidelines to the best of their ability.

Bullet splatter or fragmentation stands as the biggest downside to steel targets. Bullet splatter creates an eye hazard, so shooters should consider wrap-around eye protection crucial. When shooting steel targets, every person on the range wears protective eyewear. When using full metal jacket ammunition, large pieces of the jacket can hit a person and cause superficial nicks and cuts to the skin.

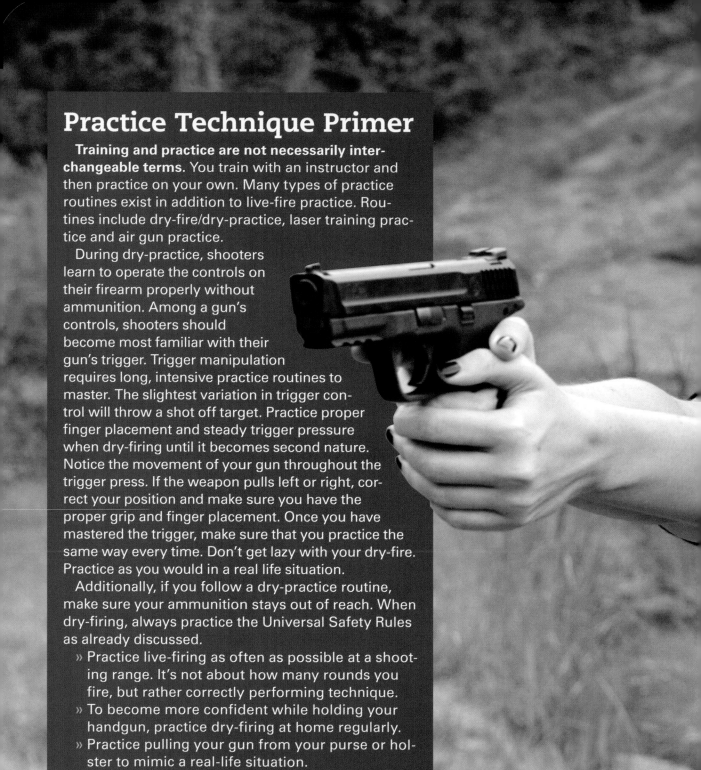

Practice Technique Primer

Training and practice are not necessarily interchangeable terms. You train with an instructor and then practice on your own. Many types of practice routines exist in addition to live-fire practice. Routines include dry-fire/dry-practice, laser training practice and air gun practice.

During dry-practice, shooters learn to operate the controls on their firearm properly without ammunition. Among a gun's controls, shooters should become most familiar with their gun's trigger. Trigger manipulation requires long, intensive practice routines to master. The slightest variation in trigger control will throw a shot off target. Practice proper finger placement and steady trigger pressure when dry-firing until it becomes second nature. Notice the movement of your gun throughout the trigger press. If the weapon pulls left or right, correct your position and make sure you have the proper grip and finger placement. Once you have mastered the trigger, make sure that you practice the same way every time. Don't get lazy with your dry-fire. Practice as you would in a real life situation.

Additionally, if you follow a dry-practice routine, make sure your ammunition stays out of reach. When dry-firing, always practice the Universal Safety Rules as already discussed.

» Practice live-firing as often as possible at a shooting range. It's not about how many rounds you fire, but rather correctly performing technique.
» To become more confident while holding your handgun, practice dry-firing at home regularly.
» Practice pulling your gun from your purse or holster to mimic a real-life situation.

Many will find laser training units with specially designed laser sensitive targets a great way to practice indoors without live ammunition. Several companies make laser conversion units for common handguns. The greatest advantage of laser training, rather than standard dry-fire, is that the user gets genuine feedback.

As with any physical endeavor, the more time you invest in practice, the better you become. If you rely on your firearm as a defense weapon, practice is critical as it eventually becomes instinctive. In a life-threatening situation, your practice sessions come into play as your adrenaline kicks in and you react on instinct.

When you practice, stay honest with yourself to discover your own shortcomings. You won't improve much by constantly doing the routines in which you excel. Instead, improve your skills by practicing what you find difficult. An amateur practices until he or she can hit the target. A professional practices until he or she cannot miss the target.

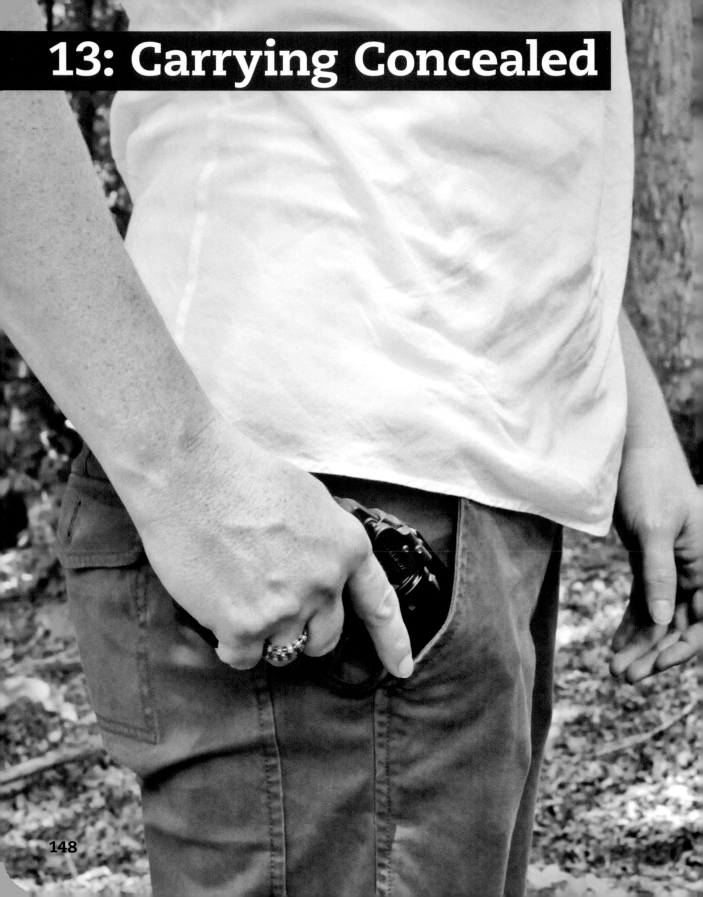

Carrying a concealed weapon is not just a choice, it's a lifestyle. This lifestyle requires careful thought before making the decision to bring a concealed weapon in public. It's not just a matter of buying a gun, but also regularly carrying it.

Carrying a concealed weapon will require some changes to your life. The most critical aspect to concealed carry is actually carrying a handgun. Locking your pistol in the trunk or glove box is useless unless you intend spending all your time in either location. If you may lawfully carry concealed and want to protect yourself and others, a handgun is required. Having a gun accessible in the car is logical when behind the wheel, but leaving your gun in the car leaves you at risk. The bottom line is simple; a handgun can only provide protection when it remains within immediate access.

Carrying a concealed weapon should become part of everyday life.

Concealed Choices

Opinions abound as to which gun to carry, but ultimately choose a gun you'll actually carry. Regardless of whether it's a revolver or pistol, each gun has its strengths and weaknesses. It's important to choose a gun you can accurately fire under stress. Many who carry concealed weapons prefer a 9mm or larger semi-automatic pistol. For revolvers, most shooters would find 38 +P as an acceptable round for concealed carry. Shooters should avoid "hand cannons," as most will find them too large to control.

Reasons for Carrying Concealed

Before carrying a concealed firearm, all those interested in carrying a concealed weapon should determine the reason driving their need for a gun. Are you carrying a gun as a piece-of-mind or for application?

Armed confrontations generally fall into two categories: shootings and gunfights. Shootings occur when one person deploys and fires a gun and the confrontation ends. The assailant either gives up, runs away or gets shot. Shootings comprise the vast majority of armed confrontations, especially for permit carriers who carry for self-protection. Gunfights fall into a different category. In gunfights, shooters exchange bullets back and forth, expending numerous rounds and can involve more than one threat.

Some will find concealed carry gives them a piece of mind more so than for actual self-defense purposes, as the likelihood of using a gun for self-defense remains small. Business owners in high-risk areas may need to defend themselves against multiple attackers, in which case a gun would serve a clearer purpose. Maybe you're a courier carrying large sums of money, jewels or other valuables and thus susceptible to armed attack.

Most will find small weapons with low capacity magazines logical choices for self defense, as most shootings involve very low round counts and single attackers. The simple presentation of a weapon may discourage an attack. Comfort can outweigh firepower, making concealment more critical than capacity. That also includes bullet size or even ease of shooting. Let's say you are carrying a pistol that's comfortable, concealable and works when needed. In this case, you use your concealed carry handgun for self-protection and not a gunfight.

How your weapon works in a fight remains more critical than its ease of carry. Your ability to use the handgun under adverse conditions should be more important than how you can conceal it. Those carrying handguns should favor guns with quality sights, longer barrels and minimal recoil. While harder to conceal, most will find larger handguns more reliable, accurate and easier to use in a fight.

A small frame semi-automatic is typically regarded as one of the best choices for concealed carry.

No matter where you conceal a handgun, make sure you can get to it quickly. It is crucial for shooters to look into their state's laws and abide by them.

A holster should allow you
to conceal the gun well,
hold it firmly in place and
keep it secure.

Holsters

Once you choose your handgun, it's time to find the proper holster for your weapon. Shooters will find even the highest quality handgun in a cheap holster uncomfortable, hard to access and even dangerous. Because of this, those carrying a concealed weapon should choose the best holster they can afford.

A quality holster should allow you to conceal the gun well, hold it firmly in place and keep it secure. A holster should hold your handgun solidly on your person and stay secure even if you find yourself forced to run. If your job or environment requires more rigorous actions, you may need a retention holster. Your handgun should never fall or slip from your holster while you carry it concealed.

Those carrying a concealed weapon should also consider investing in a gun belt. Many companies produce nice looking belts that fit into just about any clothing style. Don't choose a belt for its design, but select a belt that fits and holds your handgun.

While some may find alternate carry positions viable, most consider strong side carry the best option. Likewise, some might find ankle holsters logical for certain situations, but most will likely favor inside-the-waistband holsters best for concealed carry, as they effectively and comfortably conceal a weapon. However, those who carry larger handguns may elect to wear an outside-the-waistband holster, which provides less concealment but easier access. Those who carry very small handguns sometimes prefer pocket holsters. No matter what location or carry position, it's important for permit carriers to have easy access to their weapon.

Concealed carry is just that, concealed carry. You will need to wear clothing that conceals your handgun under normal circumstances.

What to Wear

Concealed carry is just that: concealed carry. When carrying a gun in public, you'll need to wear clothing that conceals your handgun under normal circumstances.

Most who carry a weapon find wearing loose clothing a sensible choice. Concealment is easiest in the winter when coats and outerwear can hide a gun worn on a belt or holster, though summer complicates this solution. You can also get holsters that allow you to tuck your shirt over the pistol. These holsters work well but take some practice and forethought.

If you choose an ankle rig, wear pants cut wide at the bottom. Some find vests suitable for concealed carry, but these may indicate to others that you are carrying, especially if the vest includes magazine pockets. Just remember you should try to blend in and not stick out. Most of those who carry a weapon in public will admit blending in usually becomes the biggest part of the concealed carry lifestyle. If you find yourself in a lethal encounter at a restaurant, corner store or mall, you don't want to catch an assailant's attention, but rather use surprise to your advantage.

Carrying in Public

Permit holders may find carrying in public difficult, but necessary for protection. When you go into a restaurant, get a booth. You want control, so choose a location that allows you to see the entrance and locate an exit. Booths allow you to slide in with your handgun side completely concealed. You can remove your jacket where appropriate. If possible, avoid chairs.

Follow your state's laws and make sure you can legally carry in an establishment. When you go to the restroom, take your gun with you and place it in the stall out of sight, but don't hang it on a coat hook. Instead, you should place your gun somewhere safe and secure it. Above all, make sure you place it back in your holster before leaving.

Carrying in the Car

Carry a pistol on your person even when you're in the car. Avoid placing your pistol on, in-between or under your seats. Depending on the car and your state's laws, glove boxes are also an option.

Choosing the right holster is crucial. Holsters that ride higher for access around a seatbelt are reliable. Cross-draw holsters are great for use in a car, as well as shoulder rigs. An ankle rig allows access that's not as obvious.

If your gun is in your car, secure it in a holster. When exiting your car, ensure you take your gun with you. A gun left in a car is ultimately a useless gun.

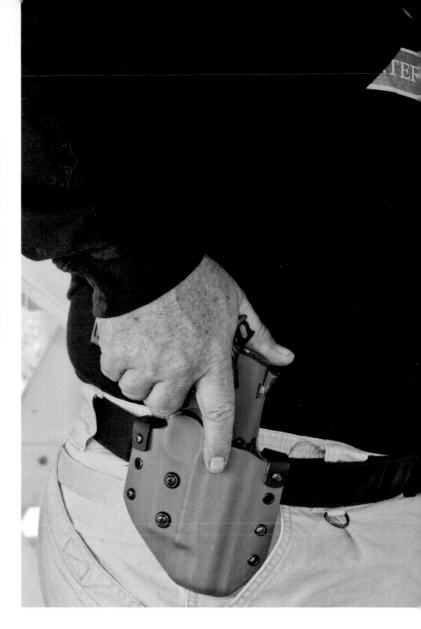

Regardless of the method of carry or the holster, you should have immediate access to the gun when needed for self-defense.

Remote Access

Those carrying a concealed firearm must practice accessing their weapon. Most will perform in the field as they practice on the range. If possible, you could even attend organized training. Organized training helps with reloading techniques, presentation, accuracy and can make you comfortable with your handgun. Training can also point out any flaws or problems with your gun, ammunition or your carry method. Some will even find local clubs and competitions worthwhile.

Carrying a concealed weapon is not just buying a gun, shooting a few rounds and storing it in a holster. All persons carrying a concealed weapon should consider how to best react to a threatening situation. Practice and training will prepare you for these real-life situations.

A prepackaged gun cleaning kit has everything needed to keep a gun clean and functional.

You have just spent the day practicing your handgun skills. That's great until inspection shows your new handgun isn't as shiny as it was this morning. Guns get dirty with use; it's the name of the game.

Rather than looks, a clean gun has far more to do with proper operation and not jamming.

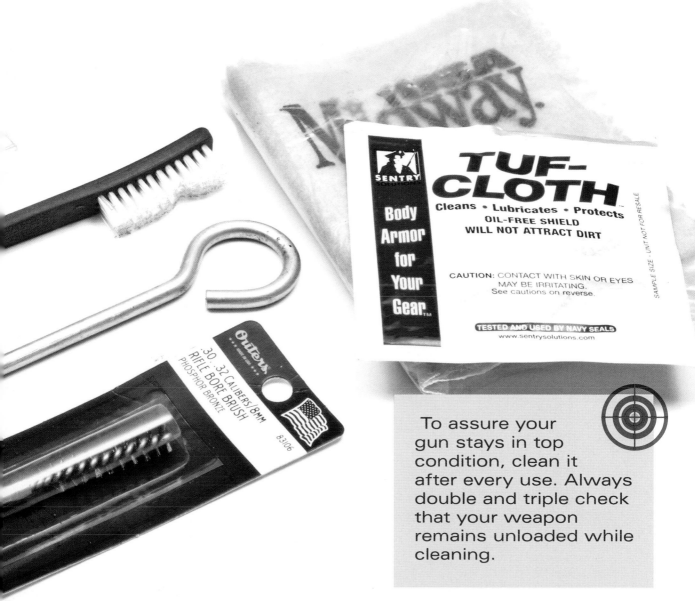

SENTRY SOLUTIONS

TUF-CLOTH

Body Armor for Your Gear™

Cleans • Lubricates • Protects
OIL-FREE SHIELD
WILL NOT ATTRACT DIRT

CAUTION: CONTACT WITH SKIN OR EYES
MAY BE IRRITATING.
See cautions on reverse.

TESTED AND USED BY NAVY SEALS
www.sentrysolutions.com

SAMPLE SIZE - UNIT NOT FOR RESALE

Outers
.30-.32 CALIBERS/8MM
RIFLE BORE BRUSH
PHOSPHOR BRONZE
83106

To assure your gun stays in top condition, clean it after every use. Always double and triple check that your weapon remains unloaded while cleaning.

Getting Dirty

Once the firing pin hits the cartridge primer, a chain reaction begins. The primer fires a small charge, which in turn ignites the main powder charge. In modern firearms, this main charge burns and creates gases that must escape the handgun. Steel surrounds the cartridge in all directions with the exception of the bore opening through the barrel. The path of least resistance allows gases to push the bullet forward. This escape of gas propels the bullet down the bore and out the end of the barrel.

This process deposits carbon, lead and copper particles in and around the bore, action and chamber of your handgun. A gun thus gets dirtier the more it's used. After a light session at the range, you may just wipe down the exterior surface and moving parts of your handgun and put it away. However, particles remain in the gun's bore and interior and will accumulate over time, potentially affecting the gun's functionality.

Long before a gun reaches that point, you need to learn how to completely remove those harmful particles and residue by giving your handgun a thorough cleaning.

A gun must be cleaned after each trip to the range to assure that it stays in top working condition.

Getting Clean

The cleaning process isn't very difficult and most gun owners find a small cleaning kit suffices in removing all unwanted residue. While gun owners can use a simple cleaning kit, every kit should include a rod that can thread through the bore and clean the inside of the barrel. Oftentimes firearm manufacturers include a cleaning rod in new guns' packaging. Any bore brush should feature either nylon or bronze bristles. These materials won't damage a gun's bore during the cleaning process, as they're softer than a steel barrel. Likewise, some of these rods may instead include a slotted tip in which a piece of cloth can attach to clean the gun's bore. You should ensure you purchase all these items in the size that accommodates your gun's barrel length and caliber. Besides various cleaning fluids, a proper cleaning kit should also include cloth patches and a cleaning brush.

To fully determine what cleaning fluids a gun requires, a shooter must establish what parts of their gun can disassemble for cleaning. Carbon deposits often cause a gun the most damage, so gun owners should clean these deposits from all detachable and accessible portions of their weapon. Luckily, most manufacturers design their cleaners to easily remove carbon.

When shopping for cleaning supplies, you'll find bore cleaners made by a host of different companies. While many brands exist, choose a brand that has thoroughly tested and researched their product and its effects on a weapon. Some shooters might even consider non-toxic lubricants and cleaners that they can safely use around pets and children.

Besides carbon, lead and copper deposits can build up in a gun as bullets pass down the bore. Lead bullets leave traces of lead, while jacketed bullets deposit copper. The speed and hardness of a bullet often determines how much lead and copper a round will leave in the barrel. Most bore solvents sufficiently remove carbon, but eliminating lead or copper deposits requires a second solvent.

Gun oil is the last essential solution needed to properly clean a gun. Once you've cleaned your gun, a coating of oil applied to all metal parts will help prevent rust and lubricate the gun's action.

Lead, copper and carbon require different solutions to clean a gun.

Cleaning Basics

Before cleaning a firearm, ensure you've unloaded the weapon. On a revolver, swing out the cylinder and visibly check for rounds. Many will find pushing the extractor a good way of double-checking for rounds their eyes might have missed the first time around. If dealing with a semi-auto, remove the magazine and pull back the slide to eject any cartridge in the chamber. Now that you've unloaded your firearm, double check and again guarantee you didn't miss a round. A little extra precaution is a small price to pay for safety.

The second step is to find a good spot to sit down and begin cleaning. You want an uncluttered location where you can set out the cleaning kit and the various parts you may remove from your firearm. A sturdy table covered by a towel or protective cover works best.

Disassembly

It's important to disassemble your handgun before cleaning so you can access the gun's internal mechanisms. Your instruction manual will show you the gun's disassembly procedures. Experts typically refer to this process as "field stripping." If you have a hard time understanding the procedure, take your handgun to a local gun shop and they can likely assist you in disassembling your gun.

Field stripping is the process of taking apart a gun for cleaning.

A proper cleaning kit should include gun cleaning fluids, cloth patches and a cleaning brush. Every cleaning kit should also have a rod to clean the inside of your barrel.

How to Clean

The actual cleaning begins by using the cleaning rod with the attached slotted tip. Take a cloth patch and run it halfway through the tip before applying bore solvent or cleaner to the patch. Apply solvent to the patch. Run the rod through the barrel a few times to coat the bore with solvent. In a semi-auto, you can clean the barrel from the chamber end after you've removed the barrel. With a revolver, you need to run the rod through each chamber in the cylinder. Once you've covered the surface with solvent, give the chemical a few minutes to sit and loosen the carbon. After a few minutes, use a clean patch to wipe out the loosened carbon. Repeating this process will completely remove all carbon residues, though lead and copper traces may or may not remain depending on the ammu-

nition used. If present, you can clean lead and copper residue in the same fashion as carbon by replacing the carbon cleaner with a lead or copper remover. Removing lead and copper will require a little extra effort. Don't forget to give the chemicals time to work between each cleaning cycle.

For stubborn deposits, you may use the bronze bore brush in the place of patches. Stainless steel brushes are also available but not advised, as they may wear down a gun's bore. Also realize that each time you fire your weapon, a certain amount of these elements collects within the bore. Each time you fire a round, the bullet will layer lead or copper over the carbon from the previous shots. Thus, you may have to alternate between the various cleaners to completely remove all traces of these three elements.

While the process sounds involved, cleaning a gun usually doesn't take long with a good set of solvents and cleaners.

Once you've cleaned the bore and chambers, it's time to address the remainder of the handgun. On a revolver, you must clean the carbon build-up on the face of the cylinder, which includes around the beginning of the barrel, known as the forcing cone. Clean these areas using a cloth patch and carbon solvent. These areas may also have traces of lead or copper deposited, which may result if the bullet scrapes the edge of the barrel as it transitions between the cylinder and barrel.

Most semi-autos require cleaning the interior of the slide. Also pay special attention to the face of the breach and around the extractor. Wipe down the surfaces along the rails of the frame and slide.

Clean the area of the feed ramp. The feed ramp guides the bullet out of the magazine and into the barrel.

Both style handguns may also require wiping down any areas where you see carbon deposits. An old cloth or a few cloth patches combined with a small amount of solvent should suit the task well.

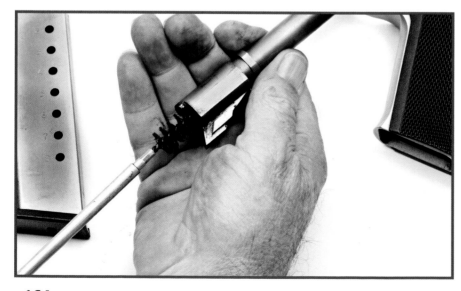

There is an advantage to being able to field strip a semi-auto. Cleaning a barrel from the chamber end reduces excess wear on the crown of the barrel.

Use the cleaning brush to reach the tight spots.

Lastly, apply a thin coat of oil down the barrel's bore and run a clean patch through to wipe off excess. On a semi-auto, you want to add oil along the rail areas on the slide and frame, as these points need adequate lubrication. Again, you could consult your owner's manual if questions about this process persist, as each should indicate points that need cleaning and lubricating.

Reassemble the firearm for the last stage of cleaning. All firearms have some metal surfaces, though some have polymer parts. These metal parts are either carbon steel or stainless steel and require some form of rust protection. Carbon steel parts have a finish or coating that helps prevent rust, so wipe these surfaces down with an oil or silicone rag after cleaning. Though stainless steel is rust resistant, you should also wipe down these guns after you've cleaned them.

During the cleaning process, many shooters often overlook the same few areas. If your handgun has removable grips, occasionally remove them to clean and lubricate the metal beneath the grips. Refrain from applying too much oil if your handgun has wood grips, as they can become saturated with oil and soften over time. Some types of lubricants or cleaners can even destroy a wood

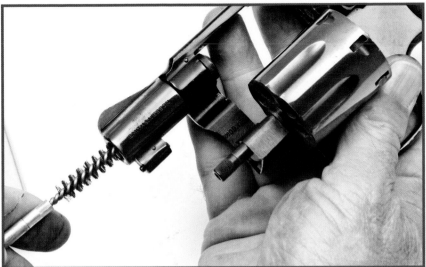

grip's finish. When cleaning semi-autos, disassemble magazines and clean them as you do your handgun. Wipe the magazines down with the silicone cloth for rust prevention. One common mistake is thinking you can't overuse or apply too much oil, but too much oil in any area where the cartridge may ride can result in a round being contaminated and rendered useless.

While cleaning a revolver, take care not to let the cleaning rod rub against the barrel crown.

Areas of carbon buildup vary between a revolver and a semi-auto handgun. The gap between cylinder and barrel allows gas to escape. Anywhere you have gas you will find dirt and grime.

Troubleshooting

Other than a good cleaning now and then, there's little the average owner must do for firearm maintenance. Should your handgun fail to fire, you can quickly check one or two things. First, if the primer shows an indention from the firing pin's striker, discard the cartridge and try another. If there isn't a sign that the firing pin struck the round, check to see if you can see any debris blocking the firing pin.

Carbon may eventually clog the interior portions of a handgun that you didn't disassemble during a normal cleaning. Most firearm problems are relatively simple to solve once the firearm is in trained hands, which would mean taking the gun to a professional gunsmith.

Over time, you will learn when the time comes for a thorough cleaning instead of a simple wipe down. It takes less time to clean your weapon than it does to wash a car, but you can benefit from a clean gun during self-defense situations.

Most gun stoppages can be cleared by visual inspection. Everything else should be taken to a professional gunsmith for proper repair.

15: Safe Storage on the Road and at Home

By its very nature, a firearm is dangerous in the wrong hands. Anyone who purchases a handgun must realize they've taken on the obligation to assure their weapon is always kept in a safe location. It's not always possible to keep the gun on your person. In fact, in many parts of the country it's also illegal. There are times when you can carry your handgun openly or concealed, but other times when you must store it at home.

Hopefully you researched all of the legalities of your home state before purchasing your firearm. You should know when and where you may carry your firearm. You should know how the state expects you to store your firearm. Remember, you're still legally responsible for your handgun when it's out of your possession.

Single occupants of a home can store a handgun unsecured and ready for immediate use. Otherwise, it must be stored in a secure location.

The glovebox might seem a logical place to store a handgun in a vehicle, but it's illegal in some states.

Traveling Storage

Traveling with a handgun creates a completely different set of conditions and additional legal issues to consider. Your local law enforcement agency can inform you of the applicable laws.

Keep in mind that crossing state lines with a handgun further complicates legal issues. Additionally, any form of public transportation, such as trains or planes, will have a set policy on how you can travel with a firearm.

When traveling in your vehicle, you must also follow certain laws and ordinances. The laws for carrying a weapon in one's vehicle and the rights of those with their concealed carry permit vary from state to state. Carry permit holders should thus determine if their state has a reciprocal agreement with other neighboring states. You can reference our book *Legally Armed: A Concealed Carry Gun Law Quick Guide* for more information regarding carrying and transporting a firearm.

Remember ignorance of the law is never an excuse and you should always research the laws of where you live and travel.

Always follow your state's laws when traveling with your handgun. Contact your local law enforcement agency for more information on your state's laws.

Storage Space

Finding the right spot and manner of storage at home may depend on whether or not you live alone. When storing your handgun, recognize that only trained adults should have access to a firearm. Even children who know how to properly handle a gun shouldn't access the weapon without adult supervision. A child may correctly handle the gun, but only an adult's maturity can determine the proper time and place to use a weapon. With that in mind, you also want quick access to your gun if you rely on it for home defense.

You may want to invest in a smaller lock box designed to hold a single handgun. Many of these lock boxes have a digital or manual combination lock that ensures only those with the combination can open it. Several handguns now come from the factory in a hard molded case that accommodates small padlocks. Additionally, some handgun owners choose to use a trigger lock to render the handgun safe, especially in a house with children. Most gun shops sell these trigger locks, which fit over the trigger or through a portion of the gun. These locks will disable the gun from firing.

Proper storage begins by following local laws. Make sure the gun is out of sight and only you can access it. Always store the gun inside a case to protect both it and you. Consider adding extra protection by using a locking device. If you're worried about getting quick access for home defense, you can practice retrieving the handgun. Start your practice with a well-lit house and practice in the dark once you become proficient in the daylight.

A padded gun case will protect your firearm from dirt and dust, but it does little to keep the handgun secure.

A simple padlock similar to a bicycle lock is all that is needed to disable a handgun.

Molded cases are becoming rather common and have the ability to be locked for secure storage.

Firearm owners should store their weapons in a secure location that they can also easily access. Many gun owners prefer a small lock box or holstered in a hidden area nearby.

Legal gun ownership is a right of all Americans. Some choose to keep their guns at home as an added measure of security and protection from intruders. Others take the right of gun ownership to a more personal level. They are part of the growing population of Americans practicing another legal right. That is holding a permit to carry a concealed weapon in public.

Concealed carry weapon permits are gaining popularity due in part to the parallel increase in violent crime. Another reason for the increase is gun manufacturers are designing handguns specifically for concealed-carry use.

Carrying a concealed weapon is legal nationwide. Some states require concealed carry weapons permit applicants to certify their proficiency with a firearm through some type of training or instruction.

The purpose of this book is to provide the basics of what to expect as the permit applicant goes through the awareness, selection and training processes required to take responsible steps toward carrying a gun in public.

Readers are encouraged to use this book as a study guide. The chapters are written to help straighten the learning curve for making the best choice when considering a gun for concealed carry use.

Review the following guidelines as you study and learn more about handgun ownership and concealed-carry weapon use. Doing so will make you a safer, more efficient shooter.

Taking an organized course led by a qualified instructor instills better core skills for handling a gun.

Take a Course

This book is not a replacement for professional instruction. Taking an organized course with others new to gun use is encouraged. The advantages of taking such a course go beyond learning the mechanics of how to operate a gun.

The social atmosphere of being surrounded by like-minded individuals instills confidence in the ability to improve shooting skills. The learning environment also provides an encouraging means of being around others who believe in the American right to legally bear arms.

A myriad of opportunities are available for learning about handgun use and applications, from self-defense to even competing in shooting sports. A starting point is the National Shooting Sports Foundation. The NSSF is widely respected for its First Shots program. First Shots helps gun ranges across the country introduce thousands of individuals to shooting and firearm safety. The program provides participants with a comprehensive introduction to shooting by qualified range operators and instructors. The course covers topics such as firearm safety, local ownership requirements, shooting fundamentals and hands-on instruction. Find out more at www.nssf.org.

Gun manufacturers are designing compact handguns specifically for concealed-carry use.

The Right Gun

When shopping for new clothes you can try them on before making a purchase. You can test drive a car before making the decision about whether or not to buy it or move on to another car dealership.

Shopping for a gun is different. You can research the choices online and even go shopping at a gun store. Talk is cheap. You can do that with very qualified professionals at the store. That is also where the first-time shopping experience ends for a newcomer to gun handling and ownership. The salesperson cannot put the gun in your hand and allow you to pull the trigger.

That is when time is well spent on a gun range with a qualified instructor or trusted friend with handgun experience. The gun range provides an organized environment for learning about gun handling and safety.

The final decision about which gun to purchase comes down to one key factor. That is choosing the one gun you are comfortable operating anywhere, anytime. The gun you carry could save your life.

Gun manufacturers recognize the spike in concealed-carry weapon permits. They are responding by designing handguns specifically for personal defense. Compact revolvers and semi-automatic pistols with laser sights are common. Many concealed-carry guns are specifically designed with the smaller hands of a woman in mind. The point is that narrowing the choices is easier than ever before.

Choose a handgun that you feel comfortable holding and can operate under any circumstance. In a bad situation, your handgun could save your life.

Safety First

Take a professional course and the first topic you will learn is about gun safety. The topic will undoubtedly resonate throughout the entire course, from beginning to end.

The reasons why are obvious. Gun safety should become second nature to the user, not unlike the reflex action that is taken when buckling up in an automobile. Learn the rules of gun safety. Those are thoroughly covered beginning on page 28 of the chapter about handgun safety.

Gun safety can never be overlooked. One slip of the mind or forgetful moment can lead to injury or worse. That is why this book ends with listing four basic rules of firearm safety.

» Always treat firearms as if they are loaded
» Always keep your finger outside the trigger guard until you are ready to shoot
» Never point the gun at anything you do not intend to shoot
» Always be sure of your target and what is beyond it

Safe shooting!

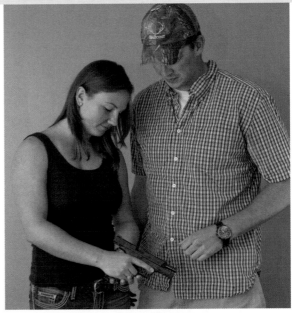

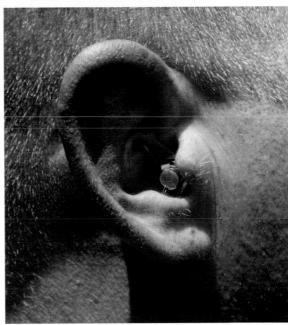

Following the basics of gun safety is a must. So is repetition of the gun rules, no matter the skill level of the shooter.

Appendix A: Manufacturers

A COMPILATION OF POPULAR HANDGUN MANUFACTURERS

Accu-Tek Firearms (Excel Industries, Inc.)
www.accu-tekfirearms.com
Excel Industries, Inc.
Corporate Office & Manufacturing Facility
1601 Fremont Ct.
Ontario California 91761
Phone: 909-947-4867

Armscor USA and Rock Island Armory
www.armscor.net
Armscor USA and Rock Island Armory
150 North Smart Way
Pahrump, NV 89060
Phone: 775-537-1444

ATI (American Tactical Imports)
www.americantactical.us
American Tactical Imports
100 Airpark Dr.
Rochester, NY 14624
Phone: 800-290-0065

Beretta USA
www.berettausa.com
Beretta USA
17601 Beretta Dr.
Accokeek, Maryland 20607
Phone: 800-929-2901

Bersa (Eagle Imports, Inc.)
www.bersa.com
Bersa
1750 Brielle Ave, Unit B-1
Wanamassa, NJ 07712
Phone: 732-493-0333

Bond Arms
www.bondarms.com
Bond Arms Inc.
P.O. Box 1296
Granbury, TX 76048
Phone: 817-573-4445

Cabot Guns

www.cabotgun.com
Cabot Gun Company LLC
799 N. Pike Road
Cabot, PA 16023
Phone: 724-602-4431

Charter Arms

www.charterfirearms.com
Charter Arms
18 Brewster Lane
Shelton, CT 06484
Phone: 203-922-1652

Christensen Arms

www.christensenarms.com
Christensen Arms
PO Box 240
550 N Cemetery Rd
Gunnison, UT 84634
Phone: 435-528-7999

Colt (Colt's Manufacturing Company)

www.coltsmfg.com
Colt Defense LLC
P.O. Box 118
Hartford, CT 06141
Phone: 800-241-2485 / 860-232-4489

CZ-USA

www.cz-usa.com
CZ-USA
P.O. Box 171073
Kansas City, KS 66117-0073
Phone: 913-321-1811

Diamondback Firearms, LLC

www.diamondbackfirearms.com
Diamondback Firearms, LLC
4135 Pine Tree PL
Cocoa, FL 32926
Phone: 877-997-6774

EAA (European American Armory)

www.eaacorp.com
EAA
P.O. Box 560746
Rockledge, FL 32956-0746
Phone: 321-639-4842

Ed Brown Products, Inc.
www.edbrown.com
Ed Brown Products, Inc.
P.O. Box 492
Perry, MO 63462
Phone: 573-565-3261

FMK Firearms
www.fmkfirearms.com
FMK Firearms, Inc.
P.O. Box 1358
Placentia, CA 92871
Phone:714-630-0658

FNH USA, LLC (FN Herstal)
www.fnhusa.com
FNH USA
PO Box 9424
McLean, VA 22102
Phone: 703-288-3500

Glock, Inc.
www.glock.com
GLOCK, Inc.
6000 Highlands Parkway
Smyrna, GA 30082
Phone: 770-432-1202

Heckler & Koch
www.hecklerkoch-usa.com
Heckler & Koch
5675 Transport Boulevard
Columbus, GA 31907 USA
Tel: 706-568-1906

Infinity Firearms
www.sviguns.com
Infinity Firearms
71229 Interstate 20
Gordon, TX 76453
800-928-1911 / 972-513-1911

I.O. Inc. (Inter Ordnance)
www.ioinc.us
I.O. Incorporated
2144 Franklin Drive NE
Palm Bay, FL 32905
Phone: 321-499-3819

Kahr Arms
www.kahr.com
Kahr Arms Factory
130 Goddard Memorial Drive
Worcester, MA 01603
Phone: 508-795-3919

Kel-Tec (Kel-Tec CNC Industries Inc.)
www.keltecweapons.com
Kel-Tec CNC Industries Inc
1505 Cox Road
Cocoa FL 32926
Phone: 321-631-0068

Kimber Manufacturing
www.kimberamerica.com
Marketing and Dealer Sales
Kimber Mfg. Inc.
30 Lower Valley Road
Kalispell, MT 59901
Phone: 888-243-4522 ext 4381

Les Baer Custom Inc.
www.lesbaer.com
Les Baer Custom Inc.
1804 Iowa Drive
LeClaire, IA 52753
Phone: 563-289-2126

Magnum Research
www.magnumresearch.com
Magnum Research, Inc. Factory
12602 33rd Avenue SW
Pillager, MN 56473
Phone: 508-635-4273

Maximus Arms, LLC
www.maximusarms.com
Maximus Arms, LLC
1226-C Lakeview Drive
Franklin, TN 37067
Phone: 615-595-9777

Nighthawk Custom
www.nighthawkcustom.com
Nighthawk Custom
1306 W. Trimble Rd.
Berryville, AR 72616
Phone: 870-423-4867

Para USA, LLC
www.para-usa.com
PARA USA, LLC.
10620 Southern Loop Blvd.
Pineville, NC 28134-7381
Phone: 704-930-7600

Remington Arms Company, LLC
www.1911r1.com
Remington Arms Company, LLC
870 Remington Drive, P.O. Box 700
Madison, NC 27025-0700
Phone: 800-243-9700

Rossi
www.rossiusa.com
Rossi
16175 NW 49 Avenue
Miami, FL 33014
Phone: 305-474-0401

Ruger (Sturm, Ruger & Co.)
www.ruger.com
Sturm, Ruger & Co., Inc.
Customer Service Department
411 Sunapee Street
Newport, NH 03773
Phone: 603-865-2442

SIG Sauer
www.sigsauer.com
U.S. Headquarters
SIG SAUER, Inc.
72 Pease Boulevard
Newington, NH 03801
Phone: 603-610-3000

Smith & Wesson
www.smith-wesson.com
Smith & Wesson
2100 Roosevelt Avenue
Springfield, MA 01104
Phone: 800-331-0852

Springfield Armory
www.springfield-armory.com
Springfield Armory
420 West Main Street
Geneseo, IL 61254
Phone: 800-680-6866

Steyr Arms (Steyr Mannicher)
www.steyrarms.com
Styer Arms
PO Box 840
Trussville, AL 35173
Phone: 205-655-8299

STI International, Inc
www.stiguns.com
STI International
114 Halmar Cove
Georgetown, TX 78628
Phone: 512-819-0656

Taurus International Manufacturing Inc.
www.taurususa.com
Taurus International Manufacturing Inc.
16175 NW 49 Avenue
Miami, FL 33014
Phone: 305-624-1115

Uselton Arms Inc.
www.useltonarms.com
Uselton Arms, Inc.
Franklin, TN 37064
Phone: 615-970-9555

Walther Arms
www.waltherarms.com
Walther Arms, Inc.
7700 Chad Colley Blvd
Fort Smith, AR 72916
Phone: 479-242-8500

Wilson Combat
www.wilsoncombat.com
Wilson Combat & Scattergun Technologies
2234 CR 719
Berryville, AR 72616
Phone: 800-955-4856

Appendix B: Organizations

A Girl and A Gun – A ladies only organization established by women shooters for women shooters with a passion for pistol, rifle and shotgun sports. The organization's mission is "to educate and encourage women about firearms usage, safety and promote women's shooting interest and participation in the competitive shooting sports."
www.agirlandagunclub.com

America's 1st Freedom – An official journal of the National Rifle Association that is focused on the constitutional right to keep and bear arms. America's 1st Freedom features the latest news concerning Second Amendment freedoms.
www.nranews.com/americas1stfreedom

American Handgunner – A magazine devoted to handguns, hunting, competition shooting, tactical knives and shooting-related activities that features reviews on guns, knives, ammunition, shooting gear, historical articles, self-defense and gun right information.
www.americanhandgunner.com

American Rifleman – A firearms publication owned by the National Rifle Association. The publication includes information on guns, newsletters, reviews, guides, galleries, video, blogs, training tips and top stories on guns.
www.americanrifleman.org

Collectors Firearms – A gun auction website with one of the largest collections of militaria, uniforms, weapons and memorabilia. Collectors Firearms features all kinds of antique and modern vintage firearms.
www.collectorsfirearms.com

Civilian Marksmanship Program (CMP) – "The Civilian Marksmanship Program is a national organization dedicated to training and educating U.S. citizens in responsible uses of firearms and air guns through gun safety training, marksmanship training and competitions." With an emphasis on youth, the CMP Mission promotes firearm safety and marksmanship training.
www.odcmp.com

Combat Focus Shooting – A program that features handgun courses and instruction with a focus on real world defense scenarios. This shooting program is "designed to help the student become a more efficient shooter in the context of a dynamic critical incident."
www.combatfocusshooting.com

Concealed Carry Magazine – A concealed and carry publication featuring crucial advice for armed citizens to better protect themselves. Includes gun and gear reviews, life-saving training, tips and answers to concealed carry questions written by leading experts on self-defense and concealed carry. Concealed Carry Magazine is a publication of the United States Concealed Carry Association.
www.concealedcarrymagazine.com

Gun Broker – "The World's Largest Online Auction of Firearms and Accessories." Gun Broker provides a secure and safe way to purchase guns, hunting and shooting accessories, while promoting responsible gun ownership.

www.gunbroker.com

International Defensive Pistol Association (IDPA) – "The International Defensive Pistol Association is the governing body of a shooting sport that simulates self-defense scenarios and real life encounters." Founded in 1996, the IDPA was formed to appeal to shooters worldwide. The organization has more than 22,000 members, representing 50 countries.

www.idpa.com

International Practical Shooting Confederation (IPSC) – "The IPSC was established to promote, maintain, improve and advance the sport of IPSC shooting, to safeguard its principles and to regulate its conduct worldwide in order to cultivate safe, recreational use."

www.ipsc.org

National Rifle Association of America (NRA) – An influential American lobbying group and large supporter of the Second Amendment. Known as "America's longest standing civil rights organization." Formed in 1871 by Union veterans Col. William C. Church and Gen. George Wingate. The NRA sponsors marksmanship events and publishes firearm based magazines such as American Rifleman, American Hunter, America's 1st Freedom, Shooting Illustrated, Shooting Sports USA and NRA Insights.

www.nra.org

National Shooting Sports Foundation (NSSF) – Known as "the trade association for the firearms industry." The NSSF promotes, protects and preserves hunting and shooting sports.

www.nssf.org

NRA Insights – An NRA publication geared towards young shooters. The publication includes stories, gun safety, games, videos, tips and pointers.

www.nrainsights.org

Second Amendment Foundation (SAF) – Strong supporter of Second Amendment rights. Promotes firearm rights through educational and legal action programs designed to inform the public about the gun control debate.

www.saf.org

Shooting Illustrated – An NRA publication that highlights firearm news, weekly polls, tips, feature stories, blogs, videos, galleries, and firearm related gear.

www.shootingillustrated.com

Shooting Sports USA – An NRA publication that focuses on competition shooting news.

www.nrapublications.org/index.php/shooting-sports-usa

Shooting for Women Alliance (SFWA) – A nonprofit organization dedicated to educate women and youth worldwide about personal defense, firearms safety, conservation and enjoyment of the shooting sports.

www.shootingforwomenalliance.com

Springfield Armory Museum – From 1777 to 1968, the Springfield Armory Museum was the primary center for the manufacture of U.S. military firearms. "The Springfield Armory National Historic Site commemorates the critical role of the nation's first armory by preserving and interpreting the world's largest historic U.S. military small arms collection, along with historic archives, buildings and landscapes."

www.nps.gov/spar/index.htm

Tactical-Life – Owned by Harris Publications, Tactical-Life is an umbrella website for the following publications: Tactical Weapons, Guns & Weapons for Law Enforcement, Special Weapons for Military & Police, Rifle Firepower, Combat Handguns, Tactical Knives, Guns of the Old West and The New Pioneer.

www.tactical-life.com

The Sportsman Channel – A television channel designed for outdoor enthusiasts with a focus on hunting, shooting and fishing for entertainment and education purposes. Known as "the leader in outdoor TV for the American Sportsman."

www.thesportsmanchannel.com

United States Practical Shooting Association (USPSA) – "The premier competitive shooting organization in the world." The USPSA site offers a club finder, articles for competitors, a rule book, match announcements and top news about the organization.

www.uspsa.org

USA Carry – A leading concealed carry online resource featuring concealed carry articles, news and training. USA Carry also features a directory where users can discover firearm instructors, gun shops, ranges and gunsmiths.

www.usacarry.com

Women & Guns – A firearms publication for women that provides information on firearms, self-defense, articles, events seminars and training information for women.

www.womenshooters.com